Discover the
Southeastern Adirondacks

Four-Season Adventures on
Old Roads and Open Peaks

Discover the
Southeastern Adirondacks

Four-Season Adventures on
Old Roads and Open Peaks

Barbara McMartin

Prepared with the assistance of Willard Reed

Backcountry Publications
Woodstock, Vermont

An Invitation to the Reader
Over time trails can be rerouted and signs and landmarks altered. If you find that changes have occurred on the routes described in this book, please let us know so that corrections may be made in future editions. The author and publisher also welcome other comments and suggestions. Address all correspondence to:

Editor
Discover the Adirondack Series
Backcountry Publications
P.O. Box 175
Woodstock, VT 05091

Library of Congress Cataloging-in-Publication Data
McMartin, Barbara
    Discover the southeastern Adirondacks.
    (Discover the Adirondack series)
    "Based upon a book originally published in 1977 under the title: Old roads and open peaks"—Verso t.p.
    Bibliography: p.
    Includes index
    1. Hiking—New York (State)—Adirondack Mountains—Guide-books. 2. Outdoor recreation—New York (State)—Adirondack Mountains—Guide-books. 3. Adirondack Mountains (N.Y.)—Description and travel—Guide-books. I. Reed, Willard. II. McMartin, Barbara. Old roads and open peaks. III. Title. IV. Series.
GV199.42.N652A3444   1986   917.47'53'043   86-10955
ISBN 0-942440-33-1 (pbk.)

Published by Backcountry Publications
A division of The Countryman Press, Inc.
Woodstock, Vermont 05091
Based upon a book originally published in 1977 under the title *Old Roads and Open Peaks* by the Adirondack Mountain Club.
Printed in the United States of America by McNaughton & Gunn
Typesetting by The Sant Bani Press
Series design by Leslie Fry
Layout by Barbara McMartin
Pasteup by Margot Powell
Maps by Richard Widhu

Photograph Credits
Ruth Rosevear, 24
W.A. Reid, 56, 87
Barbara McMartin, all other photographs
Photographs
Cover: Crane Pond from Crane Mountain's North Knob
Page 2: Crane Pond and North Knob Crane Mountain from the outlet
Page 6: Climbing Baldhead Mountain's bare rock slides

Acknowledgments

THIS UPDATED EDITION is actually the second major rewrite of the Southeastern guide. What fun it has been to revisit places I have enjoyed so much in the past, and what fun it was to discover that there are still new places to find and write about. And, best of all, many of the friends who have helped me in the past were around to walk with me this time.

I enjoyed the company and woods knowledge of Larry and Maryde King, Paul Brady, and especially Stan Pulrang, who has always been ready to go exploring at a moment's notice.

W. Alec Reid not only walked with me; he printed the photographs. James C. Dawson also accompanied me and reviewed the geological background included in the text. Dennis Conroy followed up many local contacts and explored some of the suggested canoe routes in addition to walking with me.

Willard Reed, who originally introduced me to so much of this area, rechecked many routes.

Francis B. Rosevear, who with his wife, Ruth, has explored so many historic sites, contributed the description of the ancient survey corner, section 14.

Lou Curth, who for many years covered part of this area as a DEC Forest Ranger, made several suggestions for the revised edition. He shares with me the belief that the Wilcox Lake Wild Forest could be the premier recreation area in the Southern Adirondacks. I also called on Delos Mallette, Mark Kralovic, and Steven Gunther of DEC for assistance. Also, Margaret Baldwin, DEC Cartographer, kept me apprised of the location of new state acquisitions.

Thomas Kapelewski of DEC's Northville Office and Rick Fenton of DEC's Warrensburg office helped me pinpoint any areas where conditions or management policies have changed.

Patrick Arceri brought me up to date on International Paper Company's policies on the Speculator Tree Farm.

Since the first edition of this guide, letters have brought a treasure of new material. I especially appreciate the information given me by Phyllis Tortora.

Ted Aber graciously permitted use of the material he uncovered on the Crane Mountain paint mine.

Thanks to all of them, as well as those who helped with the original guide. Without their help discovering what the area offers, I could neither cover it completely nor keep the guide up-to-date.

Contents

Waterfall, Crane Pond Outlet

Introduction

DRAW A LINE around any Adirondack region and imagine a season of walking its paths and exploring its secrets. Each area will soon reveal its intrinsic character. In the southeastern Adirondacks, you will discover a realm of open peaks with cliffs and ledges, exposed by the forest fires of nearly a century ago. You will also discover trails and bushwhacks that follow old roads, for this area was settled in the early nineteenth century. When I revisited the area to revise my earlier guidebook, I was struck by the appropriateness of that guide's title, *Old Roads and Open Peaks*.

As in the earlier guide, the open peaks lead to discussions of the region's geology as well as to the southern Adirondacks' most spectacular views. The old roads are highways leading to the stories of yesterday, forgotten settlements, tanneries, and logging operations. This is more than just a guide to the mountains and trails; it is an introduction to the social and natural history that explains the region's character.

This revised edition features activities for all seasons. The routes vary from nature paths to good climbs, from snowmobile trails to extremely difficult bushwhacks. There are adventures to please everyone. The descriptions are not so much a formal guide as an invitation to discover what lies east of NY 30 and south of NY 8, west of the Hudson and north of the Great Sacandaga Lake.

All of that region is classified as Wild Forest according to the Adirondack Park Agency State Land Master Plan. Not only is this one of the largest Wild Forest areas, it is the most varied. A wide range of activities are permitted here. The classification stems from the numerous roads that pierce the area, but these provide easy access to the deep interior. Because of its size, many parts remain as remote and primitive as those areas classified as Wilderness.

How to Use "Discover" Guides

The regional guides in this *Discover the Adirondacks* series will tell you enough about each area so that you can enjoy it any time of the year, in many different ways. Each guide will acquaint you with that region's access roads and trailheads, its trails and unmarked paths, some bushwhack routes and canoe trips, and its best picnic spots, campsites, and ski-touring routes. In addition, the guides will introduce you to valleys, mountains, cliffs, scenic views, lakes, streams, and a myriad of other natural features.

Some of the destinations are within walking distance of the major highways that ring the areas, while others are miles deep into the wilderness. Each description will enable you to determine the best excursion for you and how to enjoy the natural features you will pass, whether you are on a summer day hike or a winter ski-touring trek. The sections are grouped in chapters according to their access points; each chapter contains a brief introduction to that area's history and the old settlements and industries that have all but disappeared into wilderness. Throughout the guides you will find accounts of the geological forces that shaped features of the land. Unusual wildflowers and forest stands also will be pointed out.

It is our hope that you will find this guide not only an invitation to know and enjoy the woods but a companion for all your adventures there.

MAPS AND NOMENCLATURE

This guide includes maps derived from the Harrisburg, Lake Pleasant, Thirteenth Lake, North Creek, Lake Luzerne, and Saratoga quadrangles of the United States Geological Survey. I recommend that you purchase those maps and transfer this guide's information onto them.

Maps are available locally in many sporting goods stores. You can order maps from USGS Map Distribution Branch, Box 25286, Denver Federal Center, Denver, CO 80225. Maps are more easily obtained from Timely Discount Topos. (800-821-7609) They will send the maps the day after they receive your check or money order (no credit cards). All maps purchased through Timely Discount are on a prepaid basis only.

The names and spellings used correspond to those shown on the USGS maps; mention is made of local or traditional names that differ from the USGS.

The only confusion that may occur arises from the vagaries of the many Stony Creeks. They are all so stony that no other name would be appropriate. Stony Creek lies east of the East Stony Creek and flows into the Hudson. The East Stony Creek flows south and west into the Sacandaga.

DISTANCE AND TIME

Distance along the routes is measured from the USGS survey maps and is accurate to within ten percent. Few hikers gauge distance accurately even on well-defined trails. Distance is a variable factor in comparing routes along trails, paths, or bushwhacks.

Time is given as an additional gauge for the length of routes. It gives a better understanding of the difficulty of the terrain, the change of elevation, and the problems of finding a suitable course. Average time for walking trails is 2 miles an hour, 3 miles if the way is level and well defined; for paths, 1½ to 2 miles an hour; and for bushwhacks, 1 mile an hour.

TYPES OF ROUTES

Each section of this guide generally describes a route or a place. Included in the descriptions are such basic information as the suitability for different levels of woods experience, walking (or skiing, paddling, and climbing) times, distances, directions to the access, and, of course, directions along the route itself. The following definitions clarify the terms used in this book.

A route is considered a *trail* if it is so designated by the New York State Department of Environmental Conservation (DEC). These trails are routinely cleared by DEC or volunteer groups and adequately marked with official DEC disks. *Blue disks* generally indicate major north-south routes, *red disks* indicate east-west routes, and *yellow* disks indicate side trails. This scheme is not, however, applied consistently throughout the Adirondacks.

Some trails have been marked for *cross-country skiing*, and new *pale yellow disks with a skier* are used. *Large orange disks* indicate *snowmobile trails*, which are limited to some portions of Wild Forest Areas. Snowmobiles are permitted on them in winter when there is sufficient snow cover. Many snowmobile trails on the interior are not heavily used and can be shared by those on cross-country skis as long as the skier is cautious. Hikers can enjoy both ski and snowmobile trails.

A *path* is an informal and unmarked route with a clearly defined foot tread. These traditional routes, worn by fishermen and hunters to favorite spots, are great for hiking. A path, however, is not necessarily kept open, and fallen trees and new growth sometimes obliterate its course. The paths that cross wet meadows or open fields often become concealed by lush growth. You should always carry a map and compass when you are following an unmarked path and you should keep track of your location.

There is a safe prescription for walking paths. In a group of three or more hikers, stringing out along a narrow path will permit the leader to scout until the path disappears, at which point at least one member of the party should still be standing on an obvious part of the path. If that hiker remains standing while those in front range out to find the path, the whole group can continue safely after a matter of moments.

Hikers in the north country often use the term *bushwhack* to describe uncharted and unmarked trips. Sometimes bushwhacking means literally pushing brush aside, but it usually connotes a variety of cross-country walks.

Bushwhacks are an important part of this regional guide series because of the shortage of marked trails throughout much of the Adirondack Park and the abundance of little-known and highly desirable destinations for which no visible routes exist. While experienced bushwhackers could reach these destinations with not much more help than the knowledge of their location, I think most hikers will appreciate these simple descriptions that point out the easiest and most interesting routes and the pitfalls one might encounter. In general, descriptions for bushwhacks are less detailed than those for paths or trails, for the guide assumes that those who bushwhack have a greater knowledge of the woods than those who walk marked routes.

I have defined a *bushwhack* as any trip on which you make your way through the woods without a trail, path, or the visible foot tread of other hikers and without markings, signs, or blazes. It also means you will make your way by following a route chosen on a contour map, aided by a compass, using streambeds, valleys, abandoned roads, and obvious ridges as guides. Most bushwhacks require navigating by both contour map and compass and an understanding of the terrain.

Bushwhack distances are not given in precise tenths of a mile. They are estimates representing the shortest distance you could travel between points. This emphasizes the fact that each hiker's cross-country route will be different, yielding different mileages.

A bushwhack is said to be *easy* if the route is along a stream, a lakeshore, a reasonably obvious abandoned roadway, or a similar well-defined feature. A short route to the summit of a hill or a small mountain can often be easy. A bushwhack is termed *moderate* if a simple route can be defined on a contour map and followed with the aid of a compass. Previous experience is necessary. A bushwhack is rated *difficult* if it entails a complex route, necessitating advanced knowledge of navigation by compass and reading contour maps and land features.

Compass directions for bushwhacks are given in degrees from magnetic north, a phrase abbreviated here to *degrees magnetic*.

The guide occasionally refers to old *blazed* lines or trails. The word "blaze" comes from the French *blesser* and means to cut or wound. Early loggers and settlers made deep slashes in good-sized trees with an axe to mark property lines and trails. Later, hunters and fishermen often made slashes with knives and, though they are not as deep as axe cuts, they too can still be seen. Following an old blazed path for miles in dense woods is often a challenging but good way to reach a trailless destination. Remember, though, that it is now, and has been for many years, illegal to deface trees in the Forest Preserve in this manner.

You may see *yellow paint daubs on a line of trees*. These lines usually indicate the boundary between private and public lands. Individuals have also used different colors of paint to mark informal routes from time to time. Although it is not legal to mark trails on state land, this guide does refer to such informally marked paths.

All *vehicular traffic*, except snowmobiles on their designated trails, is *prohibited* in the Forest Preserve. There are some town roads or roads that lead to private inholdings on which vehicular use is permitted. These roads are described in the guides, and soon the DEC will start marking those old roads that are open to vehicles. Most old roads referred to in the guides are town or logging roads that were abandoned when the land around them became part of the Forest Preserve. Now they are routes for hikers, not for vehicles.

There has been an increase in the use of three- and four-wheeled off-road vehicles, even on trails where such use is not permitted. New laws will stop this use in the Forest Preserve and make sure that some of the old roads remain attractive hiking routes.

Cables have been placed across many streams by hunters and other sportsmen for crossing in high water. The legality of this practice has been questioned. Some may be safe to use, others are certainly questionable. Using them is not a recommended practice. When this guide mentions crossing streams to reach some of the hikes, you are urged to do so only when a boat can be used or in low water when you can walk across.

The *beginning of each section describing a trail* gives a summary of the distance, time, and elevation change for the trail. For unmarked routes, such information is given only within the text of each section, to allow for the great variations in the way hikers approach an unmarked route and partly to emphasize the difficulty of those routes.

Protecting the Land

Most of the land described in these guides is in the *Forest Preserve*, land set aside a century ago, where no trees may be cut. All of it is open to the public. The *Adirondack Park Agency* has responsibility for the Wilderness, Primitive, and Wild Forest guidelines that govern use of the Forest

Camping is permitted throughout the public lands except at elevations above 4000 feet and within 150 feet of water or trails. In certain fragile areas, camping is restricted to specific locations, and the state is using a new No Camping disk to mark particularly fragile spots. *Permits* for camping on state lands are needed only for stays that exceed three nights in one location or for groups of more than nine campers. Permits can be obtained from the local rangers, who are listed in the area phone books under New York State DEC.

Only dead and downed wood can be used for *campfires*. Build fires only when absolutely necessary; carry a small stove for cooking. Build fires at designated fire rings or on rocks or gravelly soil. Fire is dangerous and can travel rapidly through the duff or organic soil, burning roots and spreading through the forest. Douse fires with water, and be sure they are completely out and cold before you leave.

Private lands are generally not open to the public, though some individuals have granted public access across their land to state land. It is always wise to ask before crossing private lands. Be very respectful of private landowners so that public access will continue to be granted. Never enter private lands that have been posted unless you have the owner's permission. Unless the text expressly identifies an area as state-owned Forest Preserve or private land whose owner permits unrestricted public passage, the inclusion of a walk description in this guide does not imply a public right-of-way.

Burn combustible trash and carry out everything else.

Most *wildflowers and ferns* mentioned in the text are protected by law. Do not pick them or try to transplant them.

Safety in the Woods

It is best *not to walk alone*. Make sure someone knows where you are heading and when you are expected back.

Carry water or other liquids with you. Not only are the mountains dry, but the recent spread of *Giardia* makes many streams suspect. I have an aluminum fuel bottle especially for carrying water; it is virtually indestructible and has a deep screw that prevents leaking.

Carry a small *day pack* with insect repellent, flashlight, first aid kit, emergency food rations, waterproof matches, jackknife, whistle, rain gear, and a wool sweater, even for summer hiking. Wear layers of wool and waterproof clothing in winter and carry an extra sweater and socks. If you plan to camp, consult a good outfitter or a camping organization for the essentials. Better yet, make your first few trips with an experienced leader or with a group.

Always carry a *map and compass*. You may also want to carry an altimeter to judge your progress on the bushwhack climbs.

Wear *glasses* when bushwhacking. The risk to your eyes of a small protruding branch makes this a necessity.

Rock Summit of Crane Mountain

Do carry *binoculars* for birding as well as for viewing distant peaks.

Use great care near the *edges of cliffs* and when *crossing streams* by hopping rocks in the streambed. Never bushwhack unless you have gained a measure of woods experience. If you are a novice in the out-of-doors, join a hiking group or hire the services of one of the many outfitters in the north country. As you get to know the land, you can progress from the standard trails to the more difficult and more satisfyingly remote routes. Then you will really begin to discover the Adirondacks.

Access from the South and the Great Sacandaga Lake

THE NORTH SHORE Road of the Great Sacandaga Lake is a handsome drive past many cottages and little bays, with occasional distant views across the lake. All of the land along the shore is leased from the state and privately developed, with the exception of a few boat launching sites and the Saratoga County Park, which is near the hamlet of West Day.

The lake and its tributaries form much of three of the boundaries of the region covered in this guidebook. The lake, a man-made reservoir, had the Indian name Sac-an-da-ga, "land of waving grass," for the great grassy vly, which was flooded in 1930. Permanent acceptance of the creation of the huge flood control and power reservoir resulted in a legislated name change from "Reservoir" to the present Great Sacandaga Lake. However, because of the fluctuating water levels, it remains a reservoir and not a natural lake.

Many roads lead into the mountains north of the lake, but most give access to private land and so are not discussed in this guide. However, the many private campgrounds and lodges along the shore are ideal for a vacation near water, with the walks in this guide nearby.

The Fourth Lake Campground, which is east of the Hudson and beyond the scope of the book, would also be close to the more eastern walks.

Northampton Beach Campground on the western edge of the Great Sacandaga Lake provides camping nearest the southwestern walks.

The beaver did it

1 Beecher Creek Falls and Covered Bridge

Picnic spot

Beecher Creek Falls and its downstream covered bridge make an especially charming place to stop on a drive along the North Shore Road. The place is privately owned, but permission to visit may be obtained from Miss Nellie Tyrrell, who lives opposite the bridge. Her grandfather, Arad Copeland, built the small covered bridge in 1879 to drive his cows across the creek to pasture. The history of Beechers Hollow predates the bridge by nearly ninety years.

In the space of half a mile, the creek tumbles through a series of waterfalls and abandoned dams, relics of the early nineteenth century, when five dams harnessed the creek's water and created a miniature manufacturing complex. The Hollow's first grist mill was built in 1793. Beechers arrived in 1802. Wood from hills to the north was turned into carriages at Miss Tyrrell's great-grandfather Copeland's carriage factory. Mop wringer parts, chair rounds, carved bedsteads, handles, and rakes were all produced in the Hollow. In addition to the grist mill and the carriage factory, there were two blacksmith shops, a tannery, a mop roller factory, a rake factory, a sawmill, and a cider mill.

All the Hollow's products and others from surrounding communities are on display in a small museum dedicated to Miss Tyrrell's efforts to preserve the valley's heritage. The museum fills a one-room schoolhouse at the head of the valley, 0.5 mile east of Edinburg.

Just beyond, the North Shore Road crosses Beecher Creek and makes a sharp turn downhill. Three hundred yards east of the bridge, there is room for one or two cars to pull off the road. Here you will find a deep, cool, shaded hemlock grove between the falls and the road, perfect for a quiet moment's rest. The picnic table is higher on the slope, and the covered bridge gives access to an old road and two small footpaths on the south shore. The one leading east overlooks the stone ruins of one of the old mills.

A steep, hemlock-covered hillside shades the falls on the south, making them dark, but not so dark as to conceal the flash of cascading water as it falls over the horizontal slabs of shale. Walk along the stream just below the falls on the far side. The combination of water, deep shade, and rock permits a lush growth of mosses, unusual liverworts, and the berry bublet fern, *Cystopteris bulbifera*, which not only reproduces by spores, but also bears tiny bulblets along the fronds, which drop off to root as new plants.

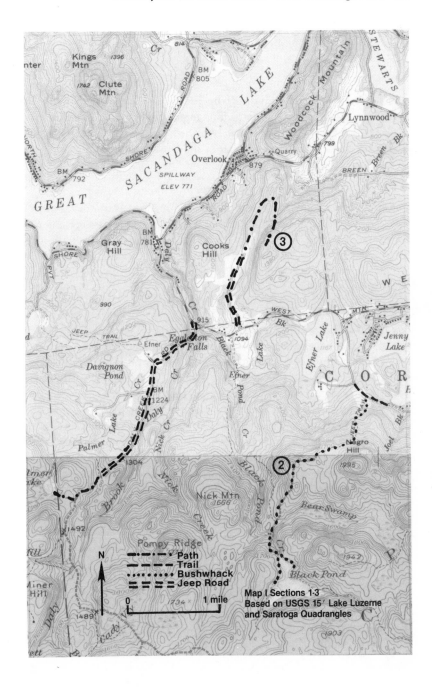

N

▬ ▪ ▬ ▪ ▬	Path
▬ ▬ ▬	Trail
• • • • • •	Bushwhack
▬▬ ▬▬	Jeep Road

0   1 mile

Map I Sections 1-3
Based on USGS 15' Lake Luzerne
and Saratoga Quadrangles

2   The Kayaderosseras Hills
Short nature walks

The range of high hills south of the Sacandaga Reservoir shelters an upland swamp known by the forbidding name of Thousand Acre Swamp. While most of the swamp is privately owned, patches of state land both north and south of it offer a number of short excursions, most leading to secluded ponds and marshes with good birding.

SPRUCE MOUNTAIN

The Spruce Mountain fire tower will not be manned because of budget cuts. The tower has been omitted from this guide in the past because its access trail is posted. There is also a road leading to the tower, which you could walk; but unless the tower is manned, you cannot enjoy the spectacular views west over Thousand Acre Swamp, south to the Catskills, north to the High Peaks, and east to Vermont.

ALBION POND

Fox Hill Road turns south from Sacandaga's South Shore Road 250 yards east of the Batchellerville Bridge. It climbs to a height-of-land at 4.1 miles. Pull off the right side of the road beside a deep hemlock forest (state owned) and walk the short path west to Albion Pond. You can easily cross its outlet beaver dam and circle the pond in less than a half hour, emerging 160 yards north of your car. At the far end of the pond, hardwood crown a sharp knob. A canoe would let you explore the marshes along the eastern shore. On the north shore a ridge separates the pond from swamps to the north.

A very handsome chain of beaver ponds along the outlet of Albion Pond is visible from Fox Hill Road as it continues south.

WEST VLY

Continue driving south on Fox Hill Road, crossing Hans and Little Hans Creeks which drain Thousand Acre Swamp. State land returns and 7 miles from South Shore Road, almost at the border of the Adirondack Park, a vehicle track forks right, west. Park and walk the 200 yards to West Vly. Unfortunately, some people use four-wheel drive vehicles for this short stretch, and treat the area as a trash dump. Barring the road will clean up the near shore, but until that is done, you can easily launch a canoe to explore the marshy shores to look for birds or to fish.

CORINTH COOPERATIVE AREA RESERVOIR

Fishing is permitted at the Corinth Reservoir, a lovely, deep, hemlock shaded body of water that is a five minute walk from County Route 10, which traverses the north end of the high mountain range. That road begins as Mosher Road heading north from NY 9N, just south of Corinth and turns into West Mountain Road as it descends to the Great Sacandaga Lake. A parking turnout for the Corinth Reservoir is 1.4 miles from NY 9N.

BLACK POND

Mesacosa Road heads south from West Mountain Road near Efner Lake, which is private. A gate bars a logging road to the west, 0.7 miles down Mesacosa Road. It leads through lumber company lands to a large patch of state land that covers Negro Hill and Black Pond. From here you can begin a walk or snowshoe trek that is 6 miles long, rises 400 feet, and takes from three to four hours. From the log staging area, several logging roads fan out, so be sure you have a map and compass for this walk. Take the more obvious road southwest, then south toward state land. It follows an old, established route, gradually uphill for a mile, then turn westerly around a shoulder of Negro Hill, where, in winter, there are fine views north.

About two miles from the start, you can still find the old cellar hole of a cabin that is reputed to have been a station on the underground railway of slavery days. Fire disturbed the area around two small hills where the road enters state land. Beyond, the old road drops down to a clearing with a hunter's cabin and crosses the outlet of Bear Swamp and then Black Pond Brook. Beyond the clearing, the route, now just a path, forks with one path leading left to the outlet of the pond, where in mid-summer there is a lush spread of pond lilies. The right path leads southeast to a more open part of the pond.

PALMER LAKE

A mile up from Brooks Bay on Sacandaga Lake, Davignon Road forks south from West Mountain Road. It crosses a high gorge over Eggleston Falls, then climbs the ridge through private lands. At 1.6 miles, a sign announces the Palmer Lake Cooperative Fishing Area. The Mettowee Lumber and Plastics Company has granted access across their lands to state land at Palmer Lake. However, no straying from the road, or camping, fishing, hunting, trapping, or use of all-terrain vehicles on their lands is permitted. Four-wheel vehicles can continue 0.5 mile farther to a parking area, but the road is so rutted it is best to park near the sign, being careful not to block the adjacent driveway.

It is an eight minute walk to the parking area on the right. The access road continues south but it is gated just beyond the parking area. Walk west through it, selecting the more traveled logging road that leads from it for another five minute walk to the lake. The walk is short enough to carry a canoe. The lake has tall standing snags of dead trees and a marshy border, ideal for bird watching.

3 Shippee's Ledge

Unmarked path, short walk or snowshoe trek
2 miles round trip, 1 hour, 260-foot vertical rise

Shippee's Ledge has a fine view of a good part of the eastern end of the Great Sacandaga Lake. To the northeast you can see Hadley Mountain Tower, in the distant west you can see Cathead. The view in mid-October is spectacular and it is an easy snowshoe trip in winter. Winds sweeping across the lake strike the cliffs, creating updrafts favored by soaring birds. A nearby resident reported sighting nine golden eagles at one time during spring migration; eagles and hawks nest nearby.

The land is private, but traditional paths have been enjoyed for many years. However, the route over the southern end of the ridge described in earlier editions has been posted so a new approach is now necessary. Note that it is possible that this approach could be closed to the public, so be very respectful of the private lands.

Turn from West Mountain Road 1.6 miles from Brooks Bay onto Shippee Road and follow it for 0.8 miles to the end. A turn-around permits you to part without blocking private driveways. The ledges are right above you. Walk north on the continuing road for about five minutes until you pass a small camp on the ledge to your right. The roadway forks 100 yards beyond the camp. Take the right fork, heading slightly downhill, circling around swamps that lie at the foot of the mountain. In three minutes there is a sharp right turn—the roadway, less obvious now, does continue straight. The right turn starts to climb the long ridge of Shippee's Ledge almost immediately. It briefly zig-zags fairly steeply, then angles right at a fork where turning left would take you across a stream. The right fork traverses west, climbing some more, then heads south and becomes more level as it approaches a height-of-land. A little more than ten minutes from the sharp right fork, watch for a cairn to the right of the path. It is just before the path climbs a short rise, after having been level for a bit. The cairn marks a path that leads 100 yards to the top of the cliffs, while the main path continues south parallel and above the ledges.

Hope Falls
and North

TAKING A WALK down many of the paths described in this guide is not simply an adventure into nature, but a step back in time. Everywhere in the Adirondacks, the paths we use today were the roads built by farmers and loggers in the 1800s. In the far southern Adirondacks, some of the paths we follow were the real highways of the nineteenth century, serving communities that disappeared many years ago. Where once there was farmland, today there is forest, and dense woods conceal almost all traces of long-deserted settlements.

Describing today's walks along these old roads would be incomplete without attempting to recreate the rugged existence of the early settlers. So this guide will follow the first settlers north from Northville, as they attempted to tame the great wilderness that today has reclaimed most of their efforts. This guide's bibliography includes the books that would help you retrace history's northward sweep as you start walking north.

This chapter starts with a walk on Mason Hill. The road over the hill led to Hope Falls, where you can still find the stone foundations of mills and tanneries. The valley along the East Stony Creek attracted farmers from all over the East. Roads from Hope Falls led northeast to Tenant Lake and northwest toward Murphy, Middle, and Bennett lakes, section 5.

When the Town of Hope was organized in 1818, it contained two communities on the Sacandaga, as well as Hope Falls, and it boasted a population of 608. Farming and the raising of sheep and cattle were soon supplanted by lumbering operations.

As early as 1805, there was a small settlement north along the Sacandaga at Pumpkin Hollow, and in 1813 a sawmill was built on Doig Creek, or Daig Creek as it is sometimes known. The main road was west from Hope Falls to Hope on the Sacandaga, then north to Wells.

By 1825, Hope Valley had two sawmills and another was constructed about three miles above Hope Falls in the 1840s. Tanneries were built there also in the 1840s. As industry flourished, the whole town grew until its population reached well over a thousand by 1880.

When synthetic chemicals for tanning were discovered and when the hillsides had yielded most of their valuable timber, the tanneries closed and the sawmills ceased operations. The population shrank to just over 300 at the turn of the century and to only 165 by 1925. When the mill dam on the East Stony Creek washed out in 1900, Hope Falls almost ceased to exist. Even the main road west from Hope Falls to the Sacandaga River was abandoned as the town diminished, and this road was not reconstructed until after 1954.

Fires swept over the mountains that had been stripped of their timber. The land could support but a few farmers. As the people left, the forest regrew to reclaim the land, leaving remnants of abandoned homes and mills along the routes of the old roads, which are now only inviting trails through the invading forests.

From the vicinity of the now flooded site of the community of Hope Valley, north along the Sacandaga to Wells, NY 30 is one of the Adirondacks' most handsome drives. South of Pumpkin Hollow, there is a view north of the cliffs on Moose Mountain, section 7. Beyond is the Sacandaga Campground, one of the state's most beautiful. It provides great camping within easy reach of the region's western day walks. Farther north, along the river, Wells is built beside man-made Lake Algonquin, which is part of the river. There are many good motels and fine places to stay in Wells, all within a short drive of the day walks that lead into these once-tamed wilds.

4 Mason Hill
Walk along an old road 4 miles round trip,
2 hours, 360-foot vertical rise

In the late eighteenth century, a few settlers reached the Sacandaga Valley near its intersection with the valleys of the East and West Stony Creeks. In 1812 a Military Road was built from the Mohawk Valley to Sackett's Harbor on Lake Ontario. A part of this road climbed north of the village of Northville, through Hardscrabble, then west to cross the East Stony Creek and continue to the Sacandaga River. This road brought settlers into the East Stony Creek Valley and the community of Hope Falls that grew up on its shores.

The old road over Mason Hill preceded by six years the road north from Hope Valley along the East Stony Creek, which is a modern roadway. The road over Mason hill is now only a pleasant walk.

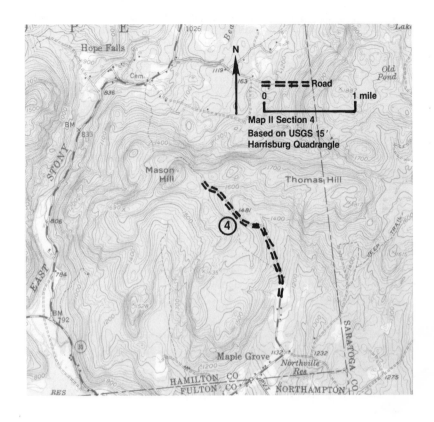

From Main Street in Northville, go east to Prospect Street and up the hill called Hardscrabble to the section known as Maple Grove. It is 1.7 miles from Northville to the Hamilton County line and 3 miles to the end of the macadam road.

The continuing dirt road is passable to four-wheel-drive vehicles, but it should be walked. Park before the end of the macadam. As the shoulders there are narrow, it may be necessary to ask permission to park of one of the homeowners near the end of the road. All the turnouts along the dirt road are posted, so do not try to park in them.

From the end of the macadam road, it is a 2-mile walk to the farm site on the top of Mason Hill. After the first 0.8 mile, the road swings from just west of north to due west and begins ascending the hill. Within 0.2 mile past the turn, there is a spring on the south side of the road. The forest has all been logged, but it is still handsome, with a variety of trees and wildflowers beneath. A swampy area to the north of the road has many plants of the deep, wet woods.

After a long, gentle climb, at 1.5 miles, stone fences of the Mason Farm begin to appear on both sides of the road. Then foundations become visible, some with trees and roots nearly concealing them. The entire hilltop is a lovely area, open in places, deeply wooded in others. Near the top, there is a small pond on the south side of the road. It is difficult to imagine that, as recently as during Civil War times, this farm was a flourishing and active place, some of whose buildings were still standing in 1939. It is even hard to picture this as a major road serving so many distant hamlets and farms, homes of the first settlers who traveled north.

There is a continuing road that loops south and is used for logging. It ends in a private yard near Maple Grove. At the top of the hill, Mason Hill Road becomes indistinguishable from other turnoffs and logging roads that lace the summit. The route was west for 0.25 mile, then north and downill toward the 1823 farmhouse, the first built in Hamilton County. Because of recent logging on the north face of the hill, the northern portion of the road has been posted, so no through trip is now possible.

5 Murphy, Middle, and Bennett Lakes

Marked trail along old roads, hiking, ski-touring
7.7 miles one way, 4¹/₂ hours, 300 feet vertical rise from the north, 520 feet from the south

While this route is marked as a snowmobile trail, there has been a road and path along most of it for over 150 years. Yellow markers also denote it as a hiking trail. Approach the lakes from either end; the most pleasant way is on a through walk from north to south. Both trailheads are on roads heading east from NY 30: Creek Road, 3 miles north of Benson Bridge over the Sacandaga, and Pumpkin Hollow Road, 4.2 miles farther north. Park at the southern trailhead, 2.5 miles east of NY 30 on Creek Road. The northern trailhead is 1.6 miles east of NY 30 on Pumpkin Hollow Road.

The trail heads south from Pumpkin Hollow Road through a pine plantation, skirting private land. Several old roadways fork right before the trail reaches state land and joins the traditional roadway south. It continues relatively level, sometimes very wet, then makes a descent to cross Doig Creek on a snowmobile bridge at 1.4 miles, about a thirty-five-minute walk. A gentle uphill follows, and at 2 miles you reach a beaver marsh with two big dams across which you see the cliffs on the mountain north of Murphy Lake. The most enjoyable part of the walk follows: a narrow draw beside the cool outlet of Murphy Lake. With a hemlock ridge to the right and the stream to the left, you climb until the trail crosses the stream and enters a rubbly draw. At 3.2 miles you reach the outlet of Murphy Lake. There is a campsite on the knoll across the outlet.

The trail continues around the north side of the lake, then swings south to the lean-to at 3.8 miles. The trail hugs the shore, but beaver have flooded three inlet streams in this stretch, creating flows that may be difficult to cross. A campsite on a hemlock knoll separates the first two marshy areas. From it are more extensive views of cliffs on the northern mountain, some that were visible from the marsh as well as of the higher range of cliffs on that same mountain. You have to jog quite far east to round the third flow, which complicates finding a good jump-off point for the bushwhack, section 6, to the top of the cliffs on the hill to the east of Murphy Lake. Flooding has impeded travel along the trail here, but it is possible to walk along the shoreline north of the lean-to. There are also lovely views from the shoreline boulders near the lean-to.

Heading south from the lean-to, it takes but fifteen minutes to walk the divide between Murphy and Middle lakes. Foundations and an old cellar hole have been found to the east of this stretch. At 4.4 miles, you reach Middle Lake where there is a good view across the water to the cliffs on the mountain to the east of Murphy Lake. Middle Lake's rock ledges lining its eastern shoreline offer good swimming. A path follows this eastern shore. The lake has an island with more ledges.

The trail follows the western shore, generally out of sight of it, but along the foot of a lovely talus slope. Ten minutes past your first approach to the lake, at about 5 miles, watch for a concealed path leading left to the south end of the lake and another lovely campsite.

Beyond Middle Lake, the trail climbs slightly, then descends, following a stream flowing into Bennett Lake. The stream descends more rapidly than the trail and shortly heads away from it. The trail descends, steeply in one section, until you see water through the trees. At 6.2 miles, about thirty-five minutes from your last approach to Middle Lake, you see a path left leading downhill to a campsite with a fireplace, outhouse and sandy beach. The trail does not go near the shore of Bennett Lake.

Five minutes past the fork to the path, watch for a sharp bend in the roadway—the marked trail takes a shortcut here. Follow the slightly longer route along the road to the right to a paint mine. At this point, opposite the southern end of Bennett Lake, a hole and a red-brown stain mark the place ferrous oxides were mined and shipped to Northville for processing

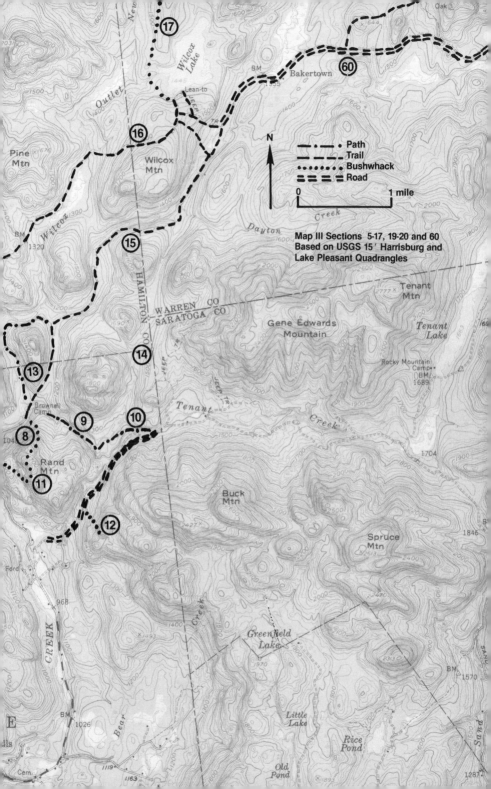

Map III Sections 5-17, 19-20 and 60
Based on USGS 15′ Harrisburg and
Lake Pleasant Quadrangles

and distribution. A small settlement grew up nearby to mine the pigment. For years, paint made from it preserved the little red schoolhouse in Hope Falls.

In the late 1800s, children of the Burgess family walked this route daily to school in Hope Falls from north of Bennett Lake. They had to leave a lantern near the road to light their way home after dark.

The 1.5 mile walk from Bennett Lake to the southern trailhead is downhill and easy. Just beyond the bend to the paint mine, a gate bars vehicular traffic from the south. However, this gate will soon have to be moved south as the state has bought the tract that stretches all the way to trailhead. The trail now follows a rutted roadway, which is often wet and muddy. After a steep pitch down, you cross a bridge at 7.6 miles, within sight of your car.

Near the lean-to on Murphy Lake

Middle Lake from the cliffs

6 The Cliffs behind Murphy and Middle Lakes
Bushwhack

If you allow an extra two hours for the through walk described in section 5, you can add an excellent short bushwhack and climb that loops 1.5 miles east of the trail. The bushwhack requires good visibility, so pick a clear day.

A valley runs just east of north from Murphy Lake, between two hills with exposed cliffs, each of which has fine views. The northern hill rises about 450 feet above the lake, with cliffs in two stages on the south face. The upper set of cliffs has nearly 100 feet of vertical rock, with fine views of the lake below. To reach them, walk east of north through the valley for ¼ mile before climbing the hill behind the cliffs to your left.

The hill to the east is another 100 feet higher, with even more spectacular views. From the very north end of the lake, climb south of east to rise above the cliffs and descend toward them. From the rock outcrops in this range, it is possible to look across the cliffs on the northern hill toward those on Moose Mountain. Cathead and surrounding mountains of the Silver Lake Wilderness are visible above the hills that border Murphy and Middle lakes on the west. Middle Lake and its island are visible from the more eastern cliff tops, as is a corner of Bennett Lake. The best treat of all is the panorama of hills to the south with the Great Sacandaga Lake beyond.

It is relatively easy to descend on the east of the summit cliffs, coming out near the outlet of Middle Lake. A word of caution: when descending these ranks of cliffs or making your way around their borders, do not go down anything unless you are sure you can continue. Climbing back up can be difficult. There are many places on this hill where there is no easy passage down the vertical rock.

7 Moose Mountain
Bushwhack walk and snowshoe trek

Moose Mountain lies opposite the Sacandaga Campground on the east side of NY 30. At present there is no trail on the mountain, though a path of sorts exists from an attempt to create a marked footpath using temporary flagging. Nevertheless, you should treat this as a bushwhack and be prepared to use map and compass to navigate the 3-mile, three-hour, round-trip climb of 860 feet. Because the face of the mountain along NY 30 is quite precipitous, the route described is the easiest one and you should use it for both the climb and the descent.

Long cliffs ring the south and southwest face of the mountain. They are topped with rock ledges from which you can view the Silver Lake Wilderness Area. The best route to the cliffs begins almost 0.5 mile south of the southerly entrance to the campground, at a point marked only by a deer crossing sign and a small rock ledge.

Enter the woods south of the ledge and head just east of north, following an intermittent stream on its north side. The stream is the outlet of a small, swampy, heavily wooded hemlock stand with a lush growth of ferns and wildflowers underneath. You reach the beginning of the hemlock swamp in ½ mile after a 350-foot climb. Follow its eastern edge curving to west of north as you pass a series of wet areas. This relatively level portion of the walk is less than ½ mile long. Following this direction, you start to climb again. Correct your route to due magnetic north.

Moose Mountain Cliffs

This route leads in ½ mile of gentle climbing to a break in the cliffs and the best place to climb above them. The break is a continuation of a small saddle on the mountaintop. To the west of the saddle there is a small opening on a cliff top. It overlooks the valley of the West Branch of the Sacandaga with views of Finch Mountain and Mt. Dunham, which edge the river's deep gorge as it exits into the main branch of the Sacandaga.

Following the top of the cliffs to the east-southeast leads to two more exposed cliffs. The entire top of the mountains is a long, thin, easily navigated ridge, which climbs gradually toward the southern summit. From the south-facing cliffs that line the ridge you can see south and southwest along the Sacandaga River, with Cathead and Wallace dominating the skyline and Three Ponds Mountain in the distance.

A fourth vantage point at the far east of the ridge provides views of the cliffs on the two hills behind Murphy and Middle lakes. The fern, rusty woodsia, which is sometimes called a resurrection fern, can be found growing in the dry mosses and lichens that edge the rock faces.

8 Brownell's Camp Trailhead
Trailhead on the East Stony Creek

The road that borders the east side of the East Stony Creek stretches 8 miles from the outlet of the creek into the Great Sacandaga Lake, through Hope Falls, and on to Brownell's Camp. The camp is a hunting lodge on a small private and posted inholding in the Forest Preserve, in the midst of what was once a huge private logging operation.

The road is designated Mudcreek Road on some maps, but this guide will refer to it as the East Stony Creek Road. Its northern, dirt-covered 2 miles are in the Forest Preserve and are occasionally difficult to drive in spring. These 2 miles make a good walk when the woods are very wet. There are several camping spots along this stretch, one large parking turnout a mile from the end, and plenty of opportunity to enjoy the accompanying creek, look for wildflowers, or watch for deer.

A large parking turnout is at the end of the road, just before the posted lands. The trailhead serves several suggested routes: a trail north-northeast to Wilcox Lake and Bakertown, section 15; a path along the East Stony, section 13; Tenant Creek Falls, sections 9 and 10; and a bushwhack to the cliffs on Rand Mountain.

Lower falls on Tenant Creek

9 Tenant Creek Falls
Picnic spot, short walk

Tenant Creek is graced with three waterfalls, and the lower one is only 0.5 miles east of the confluence with the East Stony Creek. The traditional path to the falls along the south side of the creek begins on posted land; Mr. Brownell owns 1500 feet of shoreline. Mr. Brownell suggests heading north from the parking area to cross the creek on the new snowmobile bridge and follow the north shore, thus keeping away from his buildings. If the water is low enough, you can then hop rocks back to the south side and continue to the falls on the traditional path. Alternately, you can strike out on the blazed property line, clearly marked in yellow, which follows a course of magnetic east from the parking lot. This line climbs a shoulder of Rand Mountain before dropping back to creekside and a path along the south bank to the falls.

No matter how you choose to get to the falls, it is a choice destination. The falls are nearly fifty feet tall, a high slide of water over a sloping base with a dark hemlock frame. It is an ideal picnic spot with a deep pool beneath the falls, a rich reward for such a short hike.

10 The Upper Falls on Tenant Creek
Path or walk along an old road

There are two good routes to the upper falls on Tenant Creek, it is best to combine them both into a delightful loop by walking the 2-mile stretch along the East Stony Creek Road. One leg starts as the walk to the lower falls, section 9. The beginning of the other crosses a short stretch of private land, so you will need to ask permission to cross it. Local land-owners have been generous with their permission to use this access to state land, but they do insist you ask. No vehicles or snowmobiles are permitted.

Access to state land is a dirt road on the east side and 0.4 mile south of the end of the paved portion of the East Stony Creek Road. The dirt road serves as a driveway to two houses and is barred by a chain and a sign stating it is a private road.

Bear left in 100 yards on a grassy path through an open stretch bordered by luxuriant blackberries. The road was the old route to Tenant Lake. The road jogs right in a field after five minutes, passes a barred and posted road on the right, and begins to wind up a slight grade where it enters state land. The road follows the valley between Rand and Buck Mountains, a few hundred yards up on the Buck Mountain or south side of the valley. Shortly, you enter the woods among mature hemlock and pine that impart a feeling of peace and solitude. After a moderate rise, these give way abruptly to an open area filling with birch, signalling perhaps a past forest fire. The wide, grass and needle covered roadway is soft underfoot.

After a half hour walk, past a log bridge over an intermittent stream, the track begins to hug the south side of a ravine with the hillside again studded with large hemlocks, often 2 to 3 feet in diameter. After you first glimpse Tenant Creek in the valley below, the track turns east. You cross a good bridge, then a washed out one a hundred yards farther along. Here you can turn north to follow the stream down to Tenant Creek at the third falls. If you were to continue on the roadway another hundred yards, you would reach the posted lands owned by International Paper Company, at a point that is 2 miles from the start.

The 200-yard walk through the draw and down along the small stream brings you to the third waterfall, a lively cascade that empties into a round

Pool below the upper falls on Tenant creek

pool some 40 feet across—an excellent swimming hole in high water. There is a campsite on the knoll above the falls. A narrow chute downstream is followed by rapids, then 150 yards below, the double cascades of the second falls. Its lower chute drops into a walled pool whose deep bluegreen color reflects the hemlock of the encircling ridge.

You can also reach these falls by continuing along the creek, following a fisherman's path from the falls of section 9. This way it is 1.5 miles to the upper falls, but an hour walk, compared with 2 miles and less than an hour walk along the abandoned road. A circuit using both routes is most delightful and requires about four hours.

Above the first falls, the fisherman's path hugs the shoreline, which twists and bends beneath steep, dark hemlock slopes. At one point the slopes drop so precipitously to the creek that the path climbs the ridge, follows it, then descends to stream level, thus also avoiding a huge bend in the creek. The path has been so well used that a well-defined foottread now marks the entire shore between the falls.

11 Rand Mountain Cliffs

Bushwhack

Rand Mountain is a fun mountain to climb and the bushwhack along the top of its range of cliff is relatively easy to navigate. The bushwhack begins at the end of the East Stony Creek Road, and if you combine a walk along that road with a circuit of the summit ridge, you have a wonderful 3-mile, three-hour outing.

There is a commanding view from the cliffs south along the East Stony Creek Valley toward Hope Falls, with Mason Hill beyond. Rand Mountain is not high, rising only 700 feet from the valley to a total of just 1700 feet. While the distant views are not really spectacular, they do include a glimpse of the Great Sacandaga Lake.

The walk is not a difficult bushwhack, for there are many distinguishable features to guide along the way. However, the range of cliffs is very long and quite tall. In places, it would be impossible to scale them without climbing aids, so it is wise to pay close attention to the directions in order to avoid those areas.

In all, three ranges of cliffs afford views: the west-facing cliff on the northern flanks of the mountain; the middle and longest range facing southwest; and another, lower, set on a southern shoulder of the mountain. You will see some of the cliffs as you drive north toward the mountain, so study

them to help you plan your trip.

To start the bushwhack, enter the woods to the east of the parking area at the end of the East Stony Creek Road. Follow the yellow boundary blazes east, fairly steeply uphill for about five minutes. When you see the ridge line of the Rand Mountain's flanks heading south, follow it, keeping close to the steep slopes of the escarpment that faces the west side of the mountain, but far enough back from the slopes to take advantage of the gentlest slopes. It is easy walking through the open woods. The best route is a curve southeast, then southwest.

After twenty minutes the route flattens out beneath giant hemlock, then you scale another ledge. Continuing along the ridge you meet an outcrop, which used to offer views to the northwest but now has almost filled in with striped maple and birch. Head south, crossing a draw at right angles, toward what appears to be a wall. You can find a way up it here. You reach the ridge line after a forty-five-minute walk.

Continue south along the cliff top, passing tantalizingly small openings, to a broad expanse of open rock, at 1700 feet, about sixty feet below the summit. The best views are from a precarious perch, partway down the rock face. The spot overlooks parts of the Silver Lake Wilderness with Cathead, Wallace, and Three Ponds mountains.

Rand Mountain's steep slopes are covered with pine, mixed with hemlock and spruce and an occasional burned stump of a huge tree left from logging operations many years ago. The majestic size of the forest cover is as appealing as any of Rand's views.

Note that descent along most of the southwest face is not possible. In fact you have to follow the ridge southeast for ½ mile or more in order to round the southern cliffs. A very steep descent is possible through a draw south of the summit, but it is easier to continue south until the mountain begins to fall away. It is still steep, but pick a route that traverses west. There is a level area below the cliffs, a draw of sorts. Cross it in a westerly direction, and you will come out on the lower ridge line where there are several more cliff-top vantages. You can either go south to round them, or head north along the top until you see a way down. A short, steep drop brings you to road level, about 1 mile south of the parking area.

12 Buck Mountain Cliffs
Bushwhack

As you drive south from the end of the East Stony Creek Road, look up as you round the southern shoulder of Rand Mountain. The exposed cliff, visible a little south of east on the middle of three small hills, is on a shoulder of Buck Mountain. Like Rand, Buck Mountain is faced with cliffs and steep slopes. Although they range higher than Rand's, most are so heavily wooded they offer only limited views southwest.

The summit of Buck Mountain is on the posted lands of International Paper Company, and all approaches to the mountain are on private land. However, if you have permission to use the old road access to Tenant Creek's Upper Falls, section 10, you can reach the cliffs. The view from the 1600-foot lower cliff is a limited one of the East Stony Creek Valley, but the climb to the cliff from the road is a short one. Leave the road after a walk of little more than 1 mile, and bushwhack southeast to the lower cliffs, a climb of 300 vertical feet.

13 East Stony Creek
Path, fishing, nature walk

A very easy to follow fishermen's path along the East Stony Creek can be combined with a portion of the trail, section 14, for a most rewarding short walk. Two hours will suffice for the 3-mile walk, but you will want to stop and enjoy the ferns of the deep woods and stream edge, the Canada lilies and the purple fringed orchis, and the sparkling rapids of the creek.

The snowmobile trail heads north from the East Stony Creek parking area and in 100 yards crosses Tenant Creek on a huge new bridge. On the far side of the bridge, an unmarked path leads away from the trail along the creek. If you follow it north, you will have a pleasant walk quite close to the water. Like all fishermen's routes, it gradually becomes less and less distinct. Whether following the path or bushwhacking within sight of the creek, it is a pretty walk north for 1.2 miles then east 0.4 mile to where the outlet of Wilcox Lake joins the East Stony. Less than 0.2 mile beyond that confluence, you reach the snowmobile trail as it approaches close to the creek. A walk of just over 1 mile south on this marked route completes the circuit. The return through deep forests and rich woods with a variety of ferns complements the route along the creek.

14 The North Country's Oldest Tri-County Corner

Bushwhack for history buffs

In 1683, gigantic Albany County was born, comprising all of western and northern New York and part of the present Vermont. In 1772, the oldest tri-county corner in the Adirondacks was created when the original huge Albany County was subdivided into still huge Albany, Tryon, and Charlotte counties. In 1784, these became Albany, Montgomery, and Washington, names more acceptable to the American patriots. Today, after further subdivisons, the corresponding counties are Saratoga, Hamilton, and Warren.

In 1883, the present corner was visited and identified in one of the Colvin surveys. Actually, the original corner, a "paper" corner until located and marked in Seth Baldwin's survey of 1798, is ½ mile to the north, where the present Hamilton/Warren line tops the high hill visible across "15 swamp" from Colvin's corner.

These directions are for reaching Colvin's corner, which is 1.5 straight-line miles from the parking area near Brownell's Camp, but at least twice that far by the routes suggested. Not far above the third falls in Tenant Creek, section 10, cross the creek just below the bright red paint blazes of the International Paper Company's posted property line. (At high water, crossing can be a problem.)

From the north bank of the creek, the line continues northwesterly and zigzags for almost 2 sometimes difficult miles. It is possible to stay on state land, guided by the red blazes that at first follow lot lines of Palmer's Purchase. The line goes steeply over a shoulder with frequent obstructions of thick, small growth or downed timber. It descends about as steeply to a quiet tributary of Tenant Creek, then climbs again to the first of two right-angle turns at Palmer lot corners. A third turn is at the Hope/Wells town line, which you should follow east to a corner at the Hamilton/Saratoga line.

At the first four corners there are painted stakes set in stone piles and surrounded by witness trees. (Witness trees, usually three, surround a survey corner and are blazed to point to the corner.) From the fourth corner the Hamilton/Saratoga county line is followed north ¼ mile, crossing three swampy places and coming out at the tri-county corner on the south edge of "15 swamp" (named for being in Lot 15).

The huge, ancient hemlock about which Colvin rhapsodized in his report is long ago fallen and decayed away; the corner is now marked by a painted stake surrounded by witness trees.

From the parking spot near Brownell's Camp, this route is about 7 round-trip miles, almost half cross-country. On the return trip, if darkness threatens on recrossing Tenant Creek, it is better to climb the steep south bank to the abandoned road, section 10. It is a surer and faster 2 miles, although it involves 2 additional road miles back to your car.

Study of the USGS map reveals an alternate approach to the county corner. It is off the trail to Wilcox Lake, section 15. About 1.5 miles from the bridge across Tenant Creek, the trail along the East Stony Creek is heading northeast. Here, at a double brook crossing, a bushwhack of 140° magnetic for about 0.6 mile intersects the red-blazed route east of the third of its four turns. Wherever intersected, the blazed property line can be followed left to the Colvin corner.

Wilcox Lake from the South

WILCOX LAKE IS the center of its namesake's Wild Forest Area. Each of the three separate approaches to the lake is unique, and their differences provide clues to the varied character of the terrain. The lake's heavily wooded shores are mostly spruce and hemlock groves, providing more than a half dozen good camping spots around the lake. The camper will find a lean-to at the southeastern corner of the lake. Fishermen's paths lead north from the lean-to along the east shore, past several campsites. One of the more accessible campsites is on the west shore, south of the outlet. A path swings west around the south end of the lake and follows the outlet for a time but seems to end in an alder swamp.

Beaver have been at work again, raising the level of the lake. The shoreline of this 1-mile-long lake is elongated by several bays. Wet marshes edge much of the eastern shore and wetland shrubs fill the outlet bay on the western shore. Nibbling fish and leeches make swimming from shore unattractive, but fishing remains good.

The route to the lake from the east and Harrisburg is discussed in section 60, but the character and use of that dirt road is something that the camper should not forget in planning a trip to Wilcox Lake. The road is used by four-wheel-drive vehicles all the way from Harrisburg to the snowmobile bridge over the East Stony Creek. Only beaver flooding on the creek keeps them from reaching the lake itself. Motorcycles and ATVs still reach the lake, illegally, of course, but their presence does detract from the quiet solitude you will find here during the week. Ruts from vehicles will mar the trails near the lake for a long time to come, even if vehicular use to the lake is effectively stopped. To someone who walks or backpacks the beautiful longer routes from the south and west, this vehicular use almost destroys the pleasures of the lake.

Note that the old road approach to the lake is designated as a jeep trail on the USGS. For both hikers and snowmobilers, this has been superseded by a new route, 0.3 mile south of the ford, across a new bridge, and 0.7 mile up a trail cut in the early 1970s. This bypass intersects the traditional route on a ridge, 0.2 mile from the lake.

15 East Stony Creek Trail to Wilcox Lake

Marked trail, snowmobiling, cross-country skiing, hiking, fishing, backpacking
4.8 miles one way, 2½ hours, 480-foot vertical rise

This is a route to be savored almost any time of the year. The trail passes through a deep, rich forest cover of mature trees. The creek is visible for most of the route, though the roadbed is high enough to be firm and dry. The glimpses of rapids and rocks are continually changing. In summer, Canada lilies, Joe-Pye weed, purple fringed orchis and fern-covered banks frame cascades of clear water. In winter, these cascades of silvered ice shimmer in the fading sun.

The route is marked with orange snowmobile disks and occasional old hiking trail markers. It begins at the parking area at the end of the East Stony Creek Road and heads north, crossing Tenant Creek in 100 yards. The route is east of north, through a draw between two hills, uphill at first, then level through a wet area with new planking. Maturing hemlock and fern glens highlight this first 1-mile-long stretch, which can be easily walked in twenty-five minutes.

After rejoining the creek, the trail never strays far from shoreline for almost 1.5 miles, crossing two small streams in that space. Where the steep eastern bank crowds the creek, the trail climbs 100 feet above the hemlock slopes. It then continues relatively level above the creek for 0.5 mile before descending, at 3 miles, to creek level at the point where it is joined by Dayton Creek. You will want to stop here on the bridge for pictures and a snack.

North of the bridge, the valley becomes noticeably wider, affording more distant views of surrounding hills. The 0.7 mile to the snowmobile swinging suspension bridge goes quickly, so you reach it after a total walk of no more than an hour and a half. Here you will find signs pointing straight ahead to Harrisburg Lake, 4.2 miles, and back the way you have come, Brownell's Camp, 3.7 miles. (The same distances are given at the old ford, 0.3 mile north, along with a sign giving that distance south to the bridge.)

To continue to Wilcox Lake, you will cross the bridge, wallow for a few minutes in a muddy area churned up by motorcycles, and climb 180 feet up a ridge in 0.5 mile on the trail, which now bears yellow hiking disks. Within fifteen minutes, you reach another intersection. Signs pointing west here say 4.5 miles to Willis Lake and 0.2 mile north to Wilcox Lake. The distance back says 0.5 mile to Bakertown Bridge; the distance is short and

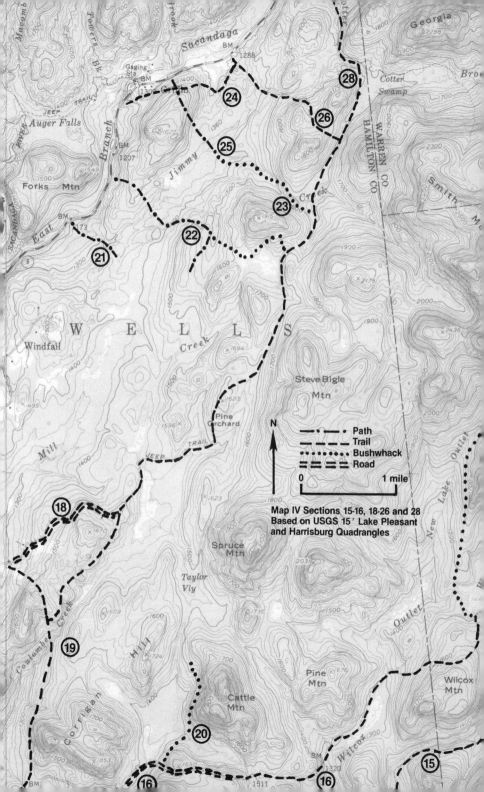

the bridge indicated is not the Bakertown one. The trail meets the old jeep road at a second intersection 200 feet beyond and you follow that rutted route for the short, sharp descent to the lake.

16 Willis Lake to Wilcox Lake

Trail, hiking, fishing
4.7 miles one way, 2 hours and 40 minutes, 520-foot cumulative vertical rise

A spectacular deep-woods walk follows this snowmobile trail, almost all of which was once an old roadway. It is the most strenuous of the three routes to Wilcox Lake, and the least used.

Two sharp pitches make it a difficult cross-country ski trail, and skiing it is currently not recommended because the crossing of Wilcox Lake Outlet is without a bridge and might be dangerous. There are no current plans to replace that bridge.

Because it is not the best way for backpackers to reach Wilcox Lake and because I think it is best enjoyed as the second leg of a trip to the lake from Brownell's Camp, the description is reversed and goes from east to west. This combination makes a great 9.5-mile day-long hike with a picnic at the lake. A word of caution: do not attempt this route if streams are running high, for crossing Wilcox Lake Outlet could be a wet affair.

To make the double trip, you will want to leave a second car at the Willis Lake Trailhead, which is 3.4 miles west of NY 30 on Pumpkin Hollow Road. That road is paved for 2 miles to the first approach to Willis Lake. Beyond, the road gradually deteriorates but is usually safe for ordinary vehicles. The parking area is just west of Doig Creek, and you will find a lovely picnic spot downhill at creekside.

To make the return here from Wilcox Lake, climb uphill from the lake to the second intersection, bearing right both times. The right fork continues to climb the shoulder of Wilcox Mountain for another 0.3 mile through an area of very old blowdown, huge decaying trunks all pointing north, relics of the 1950 hurricane.

The long, gradual downhill from the mountain is a trip into the past, for you feel as if surrounded by the primeval forest that greeted the first settlers. Patches of maturing hemlock give way to giant birch and maples

East Stony Creek

as the trail zigzags downhill. A glacial kame lies north of the trail as it descends to the valley of Wilcox Lake Outlet. You need just over half an hour for the 1.4-mile walk to the outlet. With the bridge gone, you have to hop rocks to cross the outlet, for even the huge poles that once supported the span lie at skew angles downstream.

The trail continues for almost 1 mile southwest through the level valley of the flowed lands that surround the outlet, but most of the time the flow is far enough away from the valley that you enjoy only occasional glimpses of it through the trees. In summer, you may want to detour to the flow to view the steep face of Wilcox Lake Mountain. In winter, you will certainly want to make this section of flow a part of your trek.

Enormous trees continue to shelter the route, cover so tall and stately it suggests the great climax forests that had never felt the woodsman's axe. Light filters through in streaks to dapple the low understory.

Upper East Stony Creek

Flow West of Wilcox Lake

As the flow turns south, the trail crosses an intermittent stream, turns south over a hemlock-covered knoll, and crosses a larger stream. A rise and a short, steep pitch to the southwest lead to a height-of-land in a hardwood stand. From here on the route is almost due west. A long, flat stretch follows. At 1.25 miles past the flow, you cross a creek flowing to your right. Now the trail winds about on high ground, where most trees are smaller, young hardwoods, though hemlock pockets persist and a notable stand of pine is yet to come.

As the trail reaches the final descent, signs of wear on the old road increase. The way is gravelly and steep, with old corduroy poking through. At 4.5 miles you reach the bridge and the barriers beyond. The trailhead is 0.2 mile uphill.

17 New Lake from Wilcox Lake
Bushwhack

The informal routes to New Lake from Wilcox Lake, one of which was illegally blazed in the past, seem to have faded. Perhaps the fishing is no longer an attraction.

Hunters still use the route from the private inholding south of Baker-town, though a trail marked with dull red-painted tin can lids is not as obvious as when it was used by snowmobilers. The trail made an arc north of Wilcox Lake around the southwestern flank of New Lake Mountain, toward the outlet of New Lake.

You can use a part of this route if you follow informal paths around the south end of Wilcox Lake and head northwest to cross the outlet of Wilcox Lake. Any signs of old paths in this area appear obliterated. Continue on high ground on a course just east of north for approximately 1 mile to intersect the red-marked route. When this route starts downhill to cross New Lake Outlet, you should continue north, about 100 feet in elevation above the outlet, heading east of north, gradually climbing around the west side of New Lake Mountain. You may still find signs of an old paint-blazed path, but you should consider this portion a bushwhack. The course takes you west of and below the steep slopes of the mountain, which is covered by massive hemlocks that overhang several small cliffs and boulder ledges.

As the valley becomes less steep, your course approaches the level of the outlet, in the vicinity of its intersection with a stream from Masher Vly. Follow the outlet to the lake, through wet and tangled woods and old beaver work. From this long corridor approach, New Lake appears deeply enclosed by the surrounding mountains. New Lake Mountain rises 400 feet on the south, and an even higher unnamed peak looms on the north.

New Lake is tiny and dark, with clear, cold water and thick evergreen-covered shores, so remote that it seems an almost inaccessibly distant destination. Camping spots can be found beneath the conifers, and a walk around the lake is difficult, but possible, using a combination of fishermen's paths and bushwhacks.

With luck finding the way, you should need no more than two hours for the 2.4-mile bushwhack from the lean-to on Wilcox Lake, the same for the return. If you are fortunate enough to carry a canoe or inflatable boat to Wilcox Lake, you can shorten the trip by about 0.7 mile by crossing the lake, then bushwhacking from the north end of Wilcox Lake about 200 yards inland to the red-marked route.

Trail West of Wilcox Lake

Pine Orchard

NATIVES HAVE LONG claimed the knoll known as Pine Orchard is covered with virgin pine. When dendrologists studied natural sites in the Adirondacks for inclusion in a national register, they took cores that indicated the trees date to 1815, well before the area was logged. They surmised that a natural event, perhaps a fire, but more likely a devastating hurricane known to have ravaged parts of the Adirondacks just before that date, cleared the knoll and opened it to a pioneering stand of white pine.

The origin of the stand is no more a mystery than the extraordinary girth of many of the trees. It is likely that the pine were too small to harvest when surrounding areas were logged. However, some time early in their growth, most, but not all, of the trees in the stand were attacked by either disease or insects. As a result they developed double tops and correspondingly thicker trunks. Quite a few are so large that three people with outstretched arms can not reach around them. Even the trees with single trunks are as large as thirteen feet in circumference, or four feet in diameter.

Without question, this is the Adirondacks' most accessible, awe-inspiring forest. There are two approaches to it, using trails that follow old roadways. Note that the DEC has rerouted the beginning of the snowmobile trail to Pine Orchard away from the trailhead described in section 18 in an effort to minimize contact between cars and snowmobiles. The snowmobile trail now begins on Buttermilk Hill Road east of the center of Wells. It branches from that road after a mile, winds across private land for 1.5 miles crossing south of the 1500-foot knob, crosses state land, comes close to the access road to Pine Orchard, then swings south to intersect the trail of section 19 not far north of the latter's Coulombe Creek crossing. The trail offers little for hikers or skiers, but its intersections with existing trails are noted.

18 Pine Orchard

Nature walk along an old road, ski touring
2.4 miles one way, 1 hour, minimal vertical rise

In summer, this is a favorite short walk; in winter the approach roads are not plowed, so add just over a mile and a bit of a climb to a ski trip to Pine Orchard.

To find the trailhead, drive north of Wells on Griffin Road, on the east side of the Sacandaga River, for 0.7 mile. Turn right on Windfall Road,

Forest giant at Pine Orchard

near the sight of a tannery on Mill Creek, and continue for just over 1 mile to an unmarked fork. (There have been various signs at this spot, and one occasionally identifies the right fork as Doc Flaters.) Take the right fork for 2 miles to a sign marked Visitors Parking on the right. The owner has graciously provided parking and welcomes hikers—a rare and welcome gesture—so, please do not violate his hospitality. Walk along the roadway in front of his house and into the woods. In 200 yards there is a gate at the boundary of state land. Here the trail of section 19 forks south.

The trail to Pine Orchard to the left, northeast, first passes through abandoned fields with mixed hardwoods, then beneath stands of mature spruce and hemlock interspersed with the renowned pines. The first 0.8 mile of trail is a gentle downhill leading to a snowmobile bridge. In winter, you can explore the flow both north and south of the bridge on skis.

The next 0.6 mile stretch to a second stream crossing, a washed-out bridge that should not affect your trip, is a gentle uphill with the forest growing ever taller. A sharp bend to the north takes you around the west side of Pine Orchard knoll. The tallest pine are near the crest of the hill, to the east of the trail. To the north, the trail passes through a stand of majestic hemlock, and continues to Georgia Brook, section 28.

19 Willis Lake to Pine Orchard

Marked snowmobile trail, walking, ski touring
3.5 miles one way, 2 hours, 250 feet vertical rise.

Part of this route follows old roadways, and part of it was cut to connect the Murphy, Middle, and Bennett Lakes Snowmobile Trail with the trail to Pine Orchard. It is pleasant enough to attract those out for a leisurely stroll, and if used as an approach to Pine Orchard, the 11 mile two-way trip becomes a full day outing any time of year.

The southern trailhead is 1.6 miles east of NY 30 on the north side of Pumpkin Hollow Road. Before you start, walk 100 yards east along the road to the marshy outlet of Willis Lake, an excellent spot for birding.

The trail heads north into a reforestation area, then angles east to cross Willis Lake outlet. It then jogs around private land and continues north through a high, open pine forest along an old road that is softly cushioned with a thick carpet of pine needles. However the forest has recently been broken by an extensive area of new blowdown. For 1.8 miles the route is fairly level on the west side of Corrigan Hill, until it passes right through an old foundation. In this stretch you cross two very small streams.

North of the foundation, the trail dips into the valley to cross Coulombe Creek, at the halfway point on the trip. The road disappears in the marshes north along the creek. You hop rocks to continue on the narrowly cut trail, which climbs the western slopes of a small hill above a small rock gorge. Less than five minutes past the crossing, a sign on a knoll points left to the new 3.5 mile snowmobile trail to Wells. Go straight; the trail now descends to the level of the swamps that form the headwaters of Coulombe Creek. These swamps, with their small open flows, bear the intriguing local name, the Fury Ponds. The trail climbs a ledge behind the swamps and as it descends again watch for an opening to the east; you will want to detour to explore the drying beaver meadow, a modernistic sculpture garden of starkly angled root masses.

The trail climbs into a wet draw with spagnum and large ferns. It is hard to follow the trail here—stay to the right to the end of the draw and then climb sharply away from the draw. On the next ridge, the other leg of the snowmobile trail forks back left. The trail continues climbing to a height-of-land on an open rocky knoll covered with crunchy lichens. Heading northeast along a thin ridgeline with a deep valley to the east, it passes through a handsome mixed forest, gradually descending until it reaches the Pine Orchard Trail, just east of the private lands.

The entire length boasts an unusual variety of ground covers, rich fern meadows in the deep woods and wet places, many species of *lycopodia* along the drier ridges. Pipsissiwa and wild flowers dot the route making it an ideal nature walk.

20 North of Willis Lake
Bushwhack, ski-touring

An unmarked path, undoubtedly used by hunters, heads north from the trail that connects Willis Lake and Wilcox Lake. You will find its beginning just east of the bridge over Doig Creek. The path can be followed east of north across a small stream, then north along a shoulder of Cattle Mountain. It quickly fades but can be used to approach the marshes that line the creek. In winter, you might enjoy exploring these marshes on skis.

North of Wells along the East Branch of the Sacandaga River, through Griffin, toward Johnsburg

MODERN NY 8 BRIDGES the Sacandaga River north of Wells and south of the confluence of the Main and East Branches of the Sacandaga. From the bridge northeast 18 miles to Bakers Mills, the drive along this highway is one of the Adirondacks' special treats. For two-thirds of the distance, the road follows the East Branch, with views of nearby mountains and cliffs across the rocky riverbed.

There are only four official trailheads along the road, but the dense forest that lines the route conceals a number of paths and stopping places. The main road is crossed many times by the original road, segments of which lead toward the East Branch or toward streams on the south. You will often find campers secreted in these turnouts. In places, the valley is so narrow there is barely room for the road, which is pinched between the rock-strewn river and steep mountains on the south.

Drive the road in winter and you are sure to flush a flock of evening grosbeaks pecking at the salt and sand in the road. Stop and look at ice-capped boulders in the river. In spring, snowmelt makes the water so high that whitewater enthusiasts and rafters fly down the river on waves of foam. In summer, you will ask, who pulled the plug? The river is sometimes so dry that it is a river of rock with water lying only in languid ribbons that lace the marshes. And in fall, the best time of all, the vibrant reds of swamp maples lining the shore are followed by intense yellows and oranges of birch and popple clinging to the steep mountainsides.

Work on the first sections of the road northeast of Wells began in 1839 to serve the new community of Griffin. Here, a sawmill was constructed on the East Branch, upstream from the falls. A brief history of the mill and walks in the area is given in *Discover the South Central Adirondacks*.

In 1849 the road east from Griffin, originally called the Kenyontown Road, was constructed. It was to connect Wells with the Warren County towns of Athol and Thurman, and its route was along the south side of the East Branch, through Oregon and east to Bakers Mills and Sodom to Johnsburg.

The road, now NY 8, was not improved to its present condition until nearly 1930. Until then it remained impassable at many times of the year, a great inconvenience to north country residents and a major deterrent to development in the region. This explains why this stretch of NY 8 is still a road deep in wilderness.

Where remnants of the old road persist, its intersections with the new route lead to many stopping places along the East Branch. There are also a few inviting picnic sites and intersections of the old road, looping south. One is near the Kibby Pond Trailhead leading to a small stream; another is 0.3 miles east. There is also a large picnic and parking area on the Main Branch, 0.9 mile south of the NY 8 and 30 intersection, north of Wells.

When Griffin was a thriving settlement of tanners and loggers, a number of roads were pushed south. Today they are the basis for a network of trails and paths accessible from NY 8. To make their description as simple as possible, this guide breaks them into short segments, which you will use individually or combine into longer trips.

21 Jimmy Creek Waterfall
Short path

Exactly 1 mile east of the bridge at the intersection of NY 8 and 30, Jimmy Creek flows from the south into the East Branch. There is a path along the east side of the creek for ½ mile or so. The first few hundred yards are the best because the creek cascades through a small gorge with a lovely waterfall.

The surrounding woods are rich with huge hemlocks. This is a fine picnic spot and a good place to camp not far from the road. Follow the path at least to the head of the gorge. The path continues on for under ½ mile, through swamps, along a route best suited to fishermen.

22 Jimmy Creek and Mill Creek Vly
Bushwhack, skiing

In spite of blazes and some clearing along the route, this has to be described as a true bushwhack. It leads to a flow that is fun to ski or explore on snowshoes. The route begins 0.7 mile east of Jimmy Creek. Park at the turnout on the north side of the road, and cross directly to the south to find the nearly concealed beginning of a path marked with blue and tan blazes.

The route heads east, then southeast uphill. Beyond the top of the first rise, marked with a large boulder, the blazes are infrequent especially where the path has been brushed out. If the way becomes unclear, keep the small swamp 100 feet on your left and continue on, bearing southeast.

You reach Jimmy Creek in 0.6 mile. Bear left and cross on the logs. Approximately 15 feet straight ahead of the log, there is an open path leading downstream. Follow it for about 30 feet to find a left, south, turn. Disregard the axe blazes marking a route straight ahead.

This path leads to a clearing. Since the path is very difficult to follow here, skirt the clearing to the north and east to pick up the path again. Beyond the clearing, the path goes through a small swampy area with the blazes, now yellow and tan, becoming more frequent as you proceed through it. A gentle climb follows up a ridge locally known as Sweet Ridge. Dropping down its far side, the path crosses what is, usually a dry creek bed. A rise follows, and beyond it the path enters a clearing that is filling in. Cross the clearing until you find a small maple that has a tan blaze and an old axe blaze. Head on a course of 180° into the swamp and the blue and tan blazes reappear. Follow these blazes for almost ¾ mile, through Falls Hills Swamp and up the path that ascends Falls Hill.

In this vicinity, the blazes give out entirely. Walk southwest to discover an old roadbed. The road will not be difficult to find, for it has been dug out and constructed through a 400-yard-long depressed area. The explanations for this dugway, which is at times nearly three feet deep, are intriguing and mysterious. The route is almost level. To the east, the dugway leads into Mill Creek Vly. The western section, beyond the dugway, is obliterated, but the road did reach from Windfall, and it is said that its purpose was to give access to the swamps, which were cut for hay.

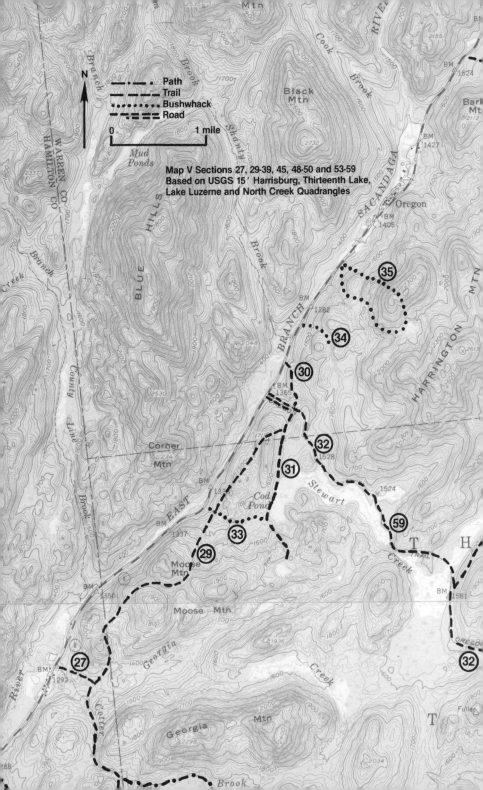

N

Legend	
—·—·—·	Path
— — —	Trail
·········	Bushwhack
—··—··—	Road

0   1 mile

Map V Sections 27, 29-39, 45, 48-50 and 53-59
Based on USGS 15′ Harrisburg, Thirteenth Lake,
Lake Luzerne and North Creek Quadrangles

The dugway is one of the few remnants of the system of roads that served the Windfall area, a place that was populated in the nineteenth century. A decade of research into the area turned up only the undocumented story that the area was once inhabited by a bunch of thieves and highwaymen about whom all that is known is their name, the Windfall Gang.

The trip to the dugway takes an hour, not allowing for time to search for blazes and consult your compass. You can either return the way you came or continue bushwhacking west along the south slopes of Oak Mountain to intersect the snowmobile trail, section 28, and follow it to make a loop back toward Griffin, or continue on the adventure described in section 23.

Fields beside NY8—former farms

23 The Upper Waterfall on Jimmy Creek
Bushwhack

It is undoubtedly easier to reach the Upper Falls on Jimmy Creek by following the route described for the end of this walk, but the trees and ferns
you will see along the way still make this trek desirable for the experienced
bushwhacker. From Falls Hill Swamp, the last place with some blazes, as
described in section 22, continue across the swamp.

You will want a route that takes you north of Mill Creek Vly and close
to the base of Oak Hill. As you find yourself heading northeast to circle
the hill, you can either head due east to intersect the trail from Pine Orchard to Cotter Brook, or you can take a detour to a special place. Watch
for a draw between the hill and a ridge to the east. It is easy to walk up
through the draw with its lush carpet of ferns. It is so open that you can
glimpse Oak Hill up on your left. The draw appears much more obvious
than the USGS indicates.

Turn southeast from the top of the draw, back toward the vly, through
a broad, rich valley. There are unbelievably thick fields of maidenhair and
Goldie's ferns and a large patch of narrow-leafed spleenwort, an uncom-
mon sight in such profusion. The wet woods support many huge trees, one
of which may be among the Adirondacks' largest elms. In this meadow,
there is also the remains of an old campsite, perhaps a hermit's den.

In this vicinity, the snowmobile route, section 28, passes close, and it
is easy to spot about 100 yards from the edge of the meadows of the vly.
If you follow the trail briefly southeast along Mill Creek, look up to the
east to discover a small cliff on the hill to the east. It is perhaps 30 feet
above the floor of the vly and 150 yards back from the place where Mill
Creek flows into the vly, and it is a good place for lunch.

Walk north on the snowmobile trail for ¾ mile, to Jimmy Creek and
bushwhack west along the creek for almost ¼ mile. Jimmy Creek enters
a deep gorge covered with beautiful hemlock and birch. Cross the creek
and continue downstream on the east side. A quarter of a mile downstream
there is another lovely gorge, with a hemlock shroud that almost conceals
the waterfall.

Continue following Jimmy Creek north. A short distance past the falls,
as the gorge containing the falls levels out, cross to the western side for
slightly easier walking. The route is still fairly brushy, but the creek is pretty
enough to compensate. About 1 mile from the falls, you approach the
meadows that surround Jimmy Creek. Cross the creek again and a tributary coming in from the northeast.

With a bit of searching about, you should be able to find the red-marked trail described in section 25 and follow it northwest to NY 8.

24 Griffin Road Connector
Marked snowmobile trail

This route was cut to connect Griffin with the snowmobile trail that continues south to Pine Orchard and to avoid a private inholding. It consists of newly cut sections at either end, with an old tote road in between. Skiers and hikers will probably want to use the more direct route described in section 26.

The trail begins 3 miles northeast of the Sacandaga Bridge on the south side of NY 8, opposite the road to Griffin Bridge. The guideboard indicating the distance to the Pine Orchard Trail is short by nearly 0.5 mile.

The trail heads due east, paralleling the road until it intercepts the tote road, here only 100 yards south of NY 8. The trail is marked along the tote road, southeast, to its end. At 0.4 mile from the start, it crosses the red-marked route of section 25. Beyond the end of the tote road, the trail has been cut for more than 0.5 mile to circle south, then north, around a large swamp. It intersects the old road to the sugarbush, section 26, within sight of the highway.

25 Jimmy Creek
Informal path, hiking, skiing, snowshoeing

Walk along the snowmobile trail of section 24 for 0.4 mile, about ten minutes. You will have to look closely, for the path is not easy to spot. It comes south from behind the old hotel at Griffin and is used by hunters. There are not good marks to indicate it, though there is an axe blaze on the northeast side of the snowmobile trail.

Assuming you have found it, turn right, or south, and you will shortly see the red blazes that mark its length. It continues over a small hill and down toward Jimmy Creek in less than 1 mile.

From here you can ski southwest along the flow or follow the creek upstream for 1 mile to the lovely Upper Falls, section 23.

26 East of Griffin, the Girard Sugarbush
Marked snowmobile trail along an old road, skiing, hiking

This route is excellent for ski-touring, but the road's history makes it equally exciting for hikers. The road led to a sugarbush where Henry J. Girard tapped 10,000 maples to produce as much as 2,000 gallons of syrup a year from 1905 until 1916, and syrup vats can still be found near the trail.

The road begins on the south side of NY 8, next to a sign directing the motorist to the large parking area 1000 feet ahead just over 1.4 miles east of Griffin. A gate bars the old roadway to all vehicles, including snowmobiles. The connector snowmobile trail, section 24, joins the roadway 100 yards from the highway. After a ten-minute walk south of NY 8, you reach a fork. The way left is another route from NY 8. You continue straight ahead.

The trail heads generally east, crossing two small streams that often overflow into the roadway, making it seem like another streambed. The road is sheltered by stands of balsam. Just short of 1 mile from NY 8, a second right fork is another old tote road that starts fairly steeply uphill. Following this route becomes a bushwhack, but it could be used to continue south to Jimmy Creek in the vicinity of the falls.

Here the trail cuts across the southern end of a small clearing. A five-minute walk beyond, less than half an hour from the road, you reach another clearing with maple syrup vats and pails. Vestiges of old tote roads converge here. Beyond the clearing, the trail heads east-southeast, uphill, for ⅓ mile, at times fairly steeply. At first only stumps of maples indicate what was the sugarbush, though higher up, a few of the giants remain. The trail levels off and follows the blazes of an old property line for 100 yards, then climbs again to the southeast. Half an hour walking from the clearing, you will see the frame of an old carriage, the spokes of its wheels partially intact.

Just beyond at a height-of-land, you can see Smith Mountain to the southeast. The route is now narrow, poorly marked. It descends briefly, then climbs again around the shoulder of a small hill, before making a short sharp descent to an intersection in the midst of a hemlock grove. It is no more than a twenty-minute walk from the last of the yellow blazes to the intersection.

Signs at the intersection indicate Georgia Brook Trailhead at 3 miles, Cod Pond at 6.6, and Willis Lake at 8.5. The signs also say it is 22.1 miles back along the route you have just followed and across NY 8 to Speculator. It is actually over 9 miles to Willis Lake, and you should add at least 1 mile to the distance given for Cod Pond.

27 Georgia Brook Trailhead

According to local custom, this is "brook," not creek as given by the USGS. The traditional Georgia Brook Trailhead was right behind Camp Georgia Brook, a very old hunter's camp. To avoid that private property, the state has made a new trailhead for snowmobiles on the other side of the brook. The trail works fine when the ground is frozen, but the area on either side of the bridge over Georgia Brook is often flooded by beaver work. Hikers either have to ask permission to use the short stretch of the old trail, risk getting wet, or make a bushwhack detour as described.

The new trailhead no longer bears the Georgia Brook name; signs denote it as the trailhead for Cod Pond and Pine Orchard. It is exactly 5 miles northeast of the Sacandaga Bridge on the south side of NY 8.

28 Georgia Brook Trailhead to Pine Orchard
Snowmobile trail, hiking, skiing
5.7 miles one way, 3½ hours, minimal vertical rise

The trail follows Georgia Brook briefly, then heads east and south for 0.4 mile to a junction. The way left goes northeast to Cod Pond, section 31, and the way right leads to Pine Orchard. (The guideboard distances are not accurate. Willis Lake Road is 11.1 miles away, 0.3 mile farther than indicated. It is 8.2 miles not to Pine Orchard, but to the Pine Orchard Trailhead. And it is 4 miles to the Cod Pond Trail, but you still have a 1-mile walk along that trail to reach the pond.)

Turn right, downhill, to reach the beaver swamp, a fifteen-minute walk from the trailhead. If the ground is frozen or it has been extremely dry, you can cross the marsh and use the bridge to cross Georgia Brook. You are apt to find 100 feet or more of flooded alder marsh on the west side of the bridge.

If it is as flooded, as it has been every time it has been visited in the past few years, you can strike out south, through a spruce swamp, and cross a small stream that comes down from Moose Mountain. Angle to the west, staying as close to the swamps as is practical, given that it is bordered by a dense spruce swamp. You reach Georgia Brook and will have to find a place where rocks and fallen logs make crossing possible. Continue west until you reach Cotter Brook (all three streams join just upstream from the bridge). Follow Cotter Brook downstream briefly to discover a log bridge that even has a railing. From the south end of the bridge, a path leads up to a seasonal hunter's camp on the slopes of Georgia Mountain. A fire, fortunately mostly a leaf fire that did not destroy mature trees, burned this area in the fall of 1985. You can use this path to explore the western slopes of the mountain. At the north of the log bridge you will find a footpath that intersects the snowmobile trail in 150 yards. The way right leads to the swamp and the infamous bridge. The trail to Pine Orchard is to the left. The detour will take a half hour to accomplish what the trail should have done in two minutes.

The trail heads briefly south, then turns west and after a ten-minute walk intersects the old roadway from Camp Georgia Brook. The way right, north, leads to that camp. You go south. The route so far has been quite handsome, in spite of the impediments. What follows is exceptionally beautiful. You climb briefly above the brook, then rejoin it at another snowmobile bridge. This one is missing a main stringer, so someone has felled—illegally, of course, but fortunately—a tree large enough to span the brook.

You will follow the brook south for the next twenty minutes, staying close as it bends to the west. The hemlock gorge that surrounds the brook grows deeper where the stream is close to the steep lower flanks of Georgia Mountain. Savor this part of the walk. Forty minutes from the flooded bridge, after 1.2 miles, the trail makes a hairpin turn. At the sharp point of the turn, a path blazed with all kinds of paint daubs heads east along Cotter Brook. It is easy to follow this path as it stays back from Cotter Swamp. The unofficial, 1-mile-long footpath leads to remote territory between Smith and Georgia mountains near the head of Cotter Swamp. The terrain is pleasant enough to invite exploration.

Since the snowmobile bridge over Cotter Brook is also out, you again have to improvise a crossing. In winter, if the flow upstream is frozen, a crossing on skis is easy. The brook has enough rocks and is narrow enough to permit a dry crossing most of the rest of the year.

The following 0.75-mile south seems longer than it is. Apparently there never was an old road or path along this route. The snowmobile trail is narrowly cut and crosses a number of small hummocks as it stays to high ground on the west side of Cotter Swamp. Skiing this stretch is not too easy. Footing is a little rough, but the handsome forest cover continues. You reach the fork to the sugarbush trail of section 26 at 2.6 miles.

A 0.75-mile level stretch takes you to Jimmy Creek, where the bridge was still standing in 1985. In the next mile, the trail swings a little east to round a small hill, then heads back southwest to cross Mill Creek. At this crossing the bridge is out, but the flow is low enough most of the year so there is no problem. If there is open water when you ski through here, detour to the northwest to the flow, which will surely be frozen so that you can rejoin the trail and continue south.

A gentle uphill of 1.4 miles takes you to Pine Orchard Knoll, described in section 18. From here it is about 2.4 miles to that Trailhead (more if it is winter) and 5.4 miles to the Willis Lake Trailhead. While both ends of this route are delightful, the middle might be considered dull and uninteresting for hikers. It rates highly, however, as a through cross-country ski trip all winter.

29 Georgia Brook Trailhead to the Oregon Trail

Marked snowmobile trail
4.4 miles one way, 2 hours, 400-foot vertical rise

The trail from Georgia Brook Trailhead to the Oregon Trail connects two great routes. At first glance, it would seem that hikers seeking to connect these routes into a long backpacking trip would also enjoy it. Such is not the case. In fact, it may be more desirable to walk along NY 8, enjoying the river, than to follow this course through a saddle of Moose Mountain, generally paralleling NY 8. At least the road provides charming views of the river and leads to lovely places to stop and just soak up the scenery.

On the south, the snowmobile trail is walked a bit as access to fishing along Georgia Creek. The rest is never walked and can be difficult to follow even though marked with orange disks. In winter some distant views are possible, but otherwise the route is featureless and dull.

30 Oregon or Shanty Brook Trailhead

The Oregon Trail begins from NY 8 immediately south of the bridge over Stewart Creek. There is room to park here. Fishermen start from this spot to try their luck in the creek.

A large parking lot, 0.45 mile north, serves snowmobilers who use the Oregon Trail or head into Cod Pond. From the parking lot, it is a fifteen-minute, 0.6-mile walk through rather nice hemlock and maple woods, south to a bridge over the creek—a lovely spot—and uphill to intersect the trail. Since hikers can reach the same spot by following the shorter, 0.3-mile, traditional roadway from the Stewart Creek Bridge to this intersection, the northern trailhead is of little use to them.

31 Cod Pond

Snowmobile trail, camping, fishing, cross-country skiing
1.2 miles one way, 40 minutes, 160-foot vertical rise

Start at the old Oregon Trailhead, and take the first right fork, 0.3 mile south, and then take a left fork, 0.2 mile later. This is the well-marked snowmobile trail to Cod Pond. The route is over the shoulder of a small hill, then almost level for the last half of the way to the shore of the pond.

Fishermen seem to camp here frequently, often right at the end of the trail. A path of sorts continues south along the pond, which is very shallow, filled with lily pads, and bordered with fairly wet shores. It certainly would be desirable to have a boat or canoe here, especially as the pond is connected with the lovely flow leading to Stewart Creek.

32 Oregon Trail to Baldwin Springs

Snowmobile trail, walking, camping, fishing, cross-country skiing
5.3 miles one way, 2½ hours, minimum vertical rise

The hub of trails at Baldwin Springs is described in Chapter IX—Harrisburg and the East Stony Creek Valley. There are many ways to reach the springs and many combinations of trails to use. Most are suitable for cross-country skiing and none are more lovely than this route, which was once the major road for settlers along the Sacandaga to trade or obtain supplies from settlements near Stony Creek.

The trail begins on the south side of Stewart Creek but swings away from the creek, reaching the intersection to Cod Pond in 0.3 mile. (Again the guideboard mileages are wrong; Baldwin Springs is 0.6 mile farther than indicated.) Continue southeast, rejoining the creek after a short walk

through delightful woods. The bridge over Stewart Creek is a mile-long, half-hour walk from the highway.

The view from the bridge across the flow is always lovely. Notice the size of the boulders in the rock causeway on the far side of the bridge, remains of an old dam. You will find several places to camp nearby.

It appears that few use the next mile or so of trail, for the way is faint. Skiers can enjoy the freedom of the open meadows rather than this narrow route. The road is far enough back from the flow to prevent summer views, but the woods are open enough to give easy access to its edge and overlooks across it to the mountains beyond.

There are enough ups and downs to make you wonder how oxen managed to pull carts through here. Rerouting to move the trail uphill from the flow accounts for the most circuitous rise, 0.5 mile from the bridge. A hundred feet from the sedge and spirea meadow, there is a small left fork that keeps to high ground. In dry weather, it is possible to follow the old route 0.25 mile across the vly before rejoining the trail. In all, the terrain is rugged enough to convince you that the trip out for salt and other staples from Oregon to Baldwin Springs was the arduous, two-day ox trip that has been recorded.

Nearly twenty minutes and 0.75 mile beyond the bridge, you may be in for a rude surprise. Beaver have dammed an arm of the flow, locally known as Rathburn Swamp, creating a large pond and a huge impediment to further progress. Of course, if it's frozen you can ski right across. Dams have a way of deteriorating quickly if untended, so the problem may diminish. With a bit of luck, you can push through alders downstream from the trail, find the long, sinuous, and not very tall dam, and walk across it to the far side without getting really wet.

As the road swings south through a wooded plain, the forest cover turns from hemlock to huge spruce and balsam and finally to pine. In the next 1.5 miles, the trail draws near the creek where it tumbles between two small hills, broken by tiny falls and rapids. The trail is briefly in a very deep, wet woods, with huge pines and the burned stumps of even larger trees. It is amazing how charring has preserved these stumps in such a wet, almost swampy woods, for this area was burned in the fires of 1903. It is also astonishing to observe the enormous size attained by the pines in the eighty years since the fires. The trail heads briefly due east across a small peninsula marked by some extraordinary pines before emerging on a big new snowmobile bridge.

Stewart Creek from the snowmobile bridge

Bridge over Stewart Creek

Across the bridge you will find an open field, a fairly popular camping spot known as North Bend. At the north edge of the field, the trail to Fish Ponds starts north. Guideboards here give this distance as 3.1 miles, short by 0.5 mile. The mileage back to NY 8, given as 2.7 miles, is also short by 0.5 mile. These signs point to the Oregon Trail straight ahead for 1.8 miles to Baldwin Springs.

You will probably appreciate the great feeling of walking though the mature forest of the past few miles even more as you continue on. Not only are the trees smaller, but the land seems much more disturbed. Signs of vehicular use increase. A gentle downhill follows. Almost 1 mile past the bridge, you see an unmarked fork to the right. It follows an old roadway generally southwest. If you have a real yen for adventure, you could use it to begin a bushwhack that would end at the path along Georgia Brook mentioned in section 28. Sportsmen also use it to begin a bushwhack to Shiras Pond.

Next on the right, beaver have flooded a meadow, making a place now full of dead trees and snags. In less than an hour from the bridge, you emerge in the fields that surround Baldwin Springs. A fork north just before the East Stony Creek also leads to Fish Ponds as well as to Garnet Lake. The official snowmobile trail, unmarked and in summer not easy to spot, continues south from the field within 100 feet of the place the road meets the creek at the ford. To continue you may need that 0.3-mile detour south to the snowmobile bridge, for a new and very large beaver dam just upstream from the bridge has flooded the creek all the way north to the ford.

33 Little Joe Pond
Bushwhack, fishing

There are unmarked fishermen's paths leading to Little Joe Pond, but since they are not easy to follow, you should consider this a bushwhack. There is no Little Joe Pond on the map; it is the name fishermen have given to the tiny pond nestled on a shoulder of Moose Mountain. Two routes lead to it. One is from the south end of the trail to Cod Pond. It goes east of south, uphill, through a draw, then swings south to drop down to the pond.

The second route begins 2.25 miles northeast of the Georgia Brook Trailhead, 1.3 miles southwest of the Oregon Trail. It has been variously marked with flags and paint daubs. After a ten-minute climb, you cross the snowmobile trail, section 29, and continue, currently guided by orange blazes, to the top of a small rise. This leads in twenty minutes to a swampy area near Cod Pond. There seems to be no obvious route to that pond, but the path now swings southeast, then due south toward Little Joe Pond. This way, the pond is only 1½ miles from NY 8, but unless you know the route, it is a difficult walk and an easy place to get lost.

34 Beaver Flow near Harrington Mountain
Bushwhack

This bushwhack begins as an unofficially marked path, 0.9 mile east of the Shanty Brook Trailhead. A red flag denotes the beginning of the path, which is easy to follow though poorly marked with a variety of yellow and white paint daubs, blazes, and red streamers. After ten to fifteen minutes of walking, you reach a clearing, an old farm settlement with a marked corner boundary and a woven wire fence that lies intact on the ground and is capable of tripping the unwary.

Just over a half hour's walk brings you to the top of a hill within view of a beaver dam and flow. Here the flags cease, indicating that some wily fisherman has used the route to his secret spot.

35 Eagle Pond and the Cliffs on Harrington Mountain
Bushwhack

Eagle is the name local people give the little pond secreted at the foot of Harrington Mountain. You may not find an eagle, but there is at least one hawk who thinks he owns the pond and will scold you for invading his territory. There once was a logging shanty on the pond, no sign of which has been found.

Two old roads, 0.1 mile apart, lie east of the Shanty Brook Trailhead. The eastern of the pair leads to an old gravel pit. The western leads to this adventure, one that must be considered a difficult bushwhack. The road begins in an open field now full of popple. Finding and staying on the road is a considerable task. After 200 yards in which the road is concealed with popple, the road begins to climb at a moderate grade, blocked with maple trees and blackberry briars. Old stumps from logging operations are visible along the way and many logs have fallen in the roadway.

The road crosses several intermittent streams, levels off, then climbs again, to end completely in what appears to be an old skidway, about 1 mile from NY 8. From here a bushwhack almost due south to the top of the hill will give you a view of the summit of Harrington Mountain. Continue just east of south down a draw on the hillside to reach Eagle Pond, where you will find several camping spots.

From the foot of the pond, bushwhack west around the hill at the same contour as the outlet, for a walk of no more than fifteen minutes. This leads to a cliff that overlooks the beaver flow of section 34 and a panorama of mountains to the south and west. There is also a ledge with views north toward Black Mountain across the East Branch.

From this point, either bushwhack a little north of west to the beaver flow and out on the route of section 34, or bushwhack north-northwest back to the start.

In addition to the cliffs with summer views, there are other cliffs with fall and winter views, suggesting a winter snowshoe trek. In winter, the easier route—through the beaver flow, then west to the ledges, and finally across to the pond—might be better than the steep trip across the hill.

36 Kibby Pond

Marked trail, fishing, camping, snowshoeing
1.8 miles one way, 50 minutes, 570-foot vertical rise

Kibby is one of the prettiest small ponds in the region, with deep, clear waters and reputedly excellent fishing. The pond is 0.5 mile long and is situated in the range of hills south of NY 8 at an elevation of 2093 feet. The views from any of its shores are pleasant, especially toward the south and Kettle Mountain. Many camping spots, all used by fishermen in spring, attest to the pond's popularity. There is a path of sorts all along the western shore. It is an ideal lake for exploring by boat, but the distance and elevation make carrying a boat here quite arduous.

The trail begins 3.7 miles northeast of the Shanty Brook Trailhead. Here the old road intersects the new NY 8, and 100 feet along the old roadway there is a small campsite that opens out and down to a stream. Cross the stream, and the path begins immediately. Yellow markers guide the way along a fairly gentle 300-foot climb up the east side of a small draw. Then, east of a level area, the path climbs southeast again before swinging due east across high ground below a small rock ledge and down to one of the hemlock- and spruce-covered campsites on the southwest of the pond.

The route is so gentle and well marked that it would provide a good snowshoe route. The actual distance appears to be shorter than the 1.8 miles stated.

37 Bartman Trailhead to Fish Ponds and on to North Bend

Marked snowmobile trail, skiing, fishing
6.6 miles one way, 3 hours, 320-foot descent

Bartman Road is 1.4 miles west of Bakers Mills and is marked with a sign pointing to the Bartman Trailhead, which is 2.6 miles south of NY 8. While it is true that snowmobile use from this trailhead has decreased in recent years, making the trails attractive to skiers, the illegal use of three-wheeled ATVs has become a very serious problem, detracting from summer enjoyment of the area.

The trail heads due south through fields returning to forest, descending gently for 0.8 mile. In the next mile, the trail drops to the level of the ponds, which is only ten feet higher than North Bend, 4.8 miles away. The way is not only steep but narrow, suitable only for experienced skiers. The rest of the way is a skier's delight. In winter, you can take advantage of the frozen meadows surrounding the ponds and Stewart Creek and the great expanse of the flow to the south.

The ponds are shallow and marshy. The walk beside them is pleasant enough, but the trail generally keeps back in the woods, offering all too few views aross the creek without leaving the trail. After 2.5 miles of level walking, watch for a left fork, the trail to Baldwin Springs, described in section 58. The area around the junction is quite overgrown and the intersection is poorly marked. The first stretch beyond the junction of the North Bend Trail is very close to the edge of the swamps through low shrubs, which have succeeded in growing over the trail and leaving it quite a mess. Within 0.5 mile, though, the trail gains higher ground and continues in high, open, handsome woods with an occasional charred stump of enormous proportion, attesting to the ferocity of the 1903 fires. The high canopy prevents the roadway from being too brushy. As you approach North Bend, the way is so open you will be convinced vehicles have used it frequently.

38 Unnamed little pond east of Bartman Road

Old road, a path and bushwhack

The local name for the pond east of Bartman Road is Davis Mountain Pond, after a Nate Davis, perhaps an early surveyor, who had a sawmill and blacksmith shop on Bartman Road. This spot, also dubbed Deserted

Stewart Creek Flow

Flow, would not survive as open water if it were not for the beaver. The old road that takes you part way to the pond is little more than a faint path now. It begins 0.2 mile north of the intersection of Bartman School Road and Bartman Road and heads east past old stone fences, apple trees, and other signs that there once was a farm here. It continues through a plantation of large pine trees and disappears. Angle south through thickening spruce. The first beaver dam you meet is out, but the next holds back a fair pond. A series of beaver dams northeast of the pond has flooded out any paths. Head south, crossing a handsome spruce-covered ledge that separates the flows from the long, thin Davis Mountain Pond.

39 Old Road south of Armstrong Road

Abandoned road, walking, snowshoeing

There is a big bend in Bartman Road 1 mile south of NY 8. Armstrong Road heads southwest, 0.2 mile south of the bend, and leads 2.25 miles to Garnet Lake Road. About 1.3 miles south of Bartman Road, Armstrong Road passes over a small stream and a wet area with a handsome stand of ferns. Within 50 yards of the wet area, a road branches off to the left, north, up a hill to a private house. Just 200 feet south of this private road, on the south side of the road, at a place marked by an old apple tree, the old road south begins. It is one of the better old roads for walking and appears as a trail on recent USGS maps. On the 1898 surveys it is shown as a road leading to five houses that were spread out along the western slopes of Buck Hill. It was known as Sheffer Road for the family that lived in a clearing near the end of the road.

Begin by crossing a small creek, a tributary of Mill Creek, just downstream from the tumbledown old log bridge. Go up the far bank and walk straight through the brambles and tall grass for 45 to 50 paces from the stream; then turn left, or south. The road is not visible at this point as young poplar have grown to fifteen feet in height. If you keep walking south on the level, you will come to it within 100 yards. You will pass two clear logging roads that go uphill, but do not take them. Stay parallel to the brook.

All signs of logging end after 300 yards, and the old road continues on public land. It makes a gentle, uphill climb along a firmly constructed base, graded with stones on the downhill side. The climb is through mixed hardwoods, punctuated by the frosty white of huge paper birch. The trees are at first very small, perhaps because of the lack of water on the steeper slopes. The road crosses five small streams, only the last two of which have springs or any summer water. You wonder how the early settlers survived. Was it possible the water shortage did not become acute until the drought of the early 1900s and the subsequent fires that so altered the mountain's water-holding capacity?

The road levels off after 1.25 miles and continues through an area of beautiful hemlocks. Near the end of the road, there is a plantation of large pines. A field of blackberries and brambles marks the end of the road. This was the site of the Sheffer farm, and to the southwest of the field there is a small spring-fed stream and a garbage pit filled with very old tin cans.

The remoteness of the walk underscores the ruggedness of the early settlers. The forests have so overgrown the other homesites that only one is obvious. The well-constructed old road makes an excellent packed walking surface, and after the overgrown beginning, the route is so easy to follow that it would be suitable for hikers with minimal woods experience.

The way is gentle and easy, and the summer hints of views of Ross Mountain are sufficiently inviting that this route would be perfect for a snowshoe trip. In fact, a more rugged, circular winter walk is suggested, using two cars if needed. You could snowshoe due west from the homesite at the end of the road through the draw created by a small stream, ½ mile to a small pond. After crossing it, follow its outlet a little south of west to the Fish Ponds snowmobile trail, which will lead you back to the Bartman Trailhead.

Open Peaks

THE ENTIRE EASTERN range of the southern Adirondacks is spectacularly open, with many opportunities for climbing. Because the top quarter or so of many mountains is partially bare, you frequently encounter magnificent overlooks on climbs along the exposed rock, as well as at the summits. The mountains west of the Hudson are domelike and steep-sided, often rising in isolated splendor more than a thousand or fifteen hundred feet above the surrounding valleys. Only a few long ridges mark the area. The 9-mile ridge of West Mountain, with Hadley and Roundtop dominant, is the largest, twice the length of the next longest ridge.

The mountains are formed of metamorphosed sedimentary rocks interspersed with coarsely crystalline igneous rocks that have been metamorphosed to form gneisses. The building of these mountains is discussed in more detail in the section on Crane Mountain, but it was two other sequences of events that account for the openness of the peaks, whose summits are all below timberline.

The Adirondacks were buried several times by ice sheets, with the last glacier retreating about fourteen thousand years ago. Evidence of glacial activity is found everywhere—in the striations scratched on exposed rocks, in the scattered glacial boulders called erratics, and in the sandy outwash plains found in the valleys between the mountains. Huge erratics can even be found near the tops of the highest peaks, where an occasional improbably placed balancing rock perches on an open summit.

The domes were all scraped by the advancing glaciers, with the last major sheet moving from northeast to southwest. This left gentle northern slopes and steeply eroded, gouged southern faces. Glacial ground moraine material, a mixture of clay, sand, gravel, and boulders known as till, was deposited by the advancing sheets more heavily on the northern slopes, while the southern faces were left with the steep cliffs we see today.

The glacial tills were slowly covered with vegetation, and in the valleys, or on the northern slopes, a layer of decayed plants accumulated, creating rich top soil. On the steeper slopes, only lichens and mosses could gain a foothold on the bare rock, with pioneering trees sending roots into cracks in the cliffs. However, even on the steepest cliffs, some soil did accumulate, so that by the time the first settlers arrived, there was an almost continuous forest cover, broken only by beaver meadows and marshes—places too wet to sustain trees.

Some slopes were covered with pioneering vegetation—birch, striped maple and balsam—the same trees that struggle today to reclaim bare mountain tops. But most of the forests were a high open mixture of hardwoods and evergreens, similar to the deep woods of today except for the greater preponderance of evergreens and more numerous stands of giant pines.

It took a second series of events, after the glaciers, to alter the forested peaks and make them so desirable for climbing. That sequence began with the lumbering that denuded most of the mountain peaks during the nineteenth century. Some of the woods were cleared to create small farms, but the vast majority of the cutting was done to harvest the precious timber.

The valuable pines were the first to go. Next, the hemlocks were cut and stripped of their bark for tanning. The logs were often left in the woods to rot. Finally, all accessible areas were logged for building material and pulp wood for paper.

By the 1880s, much of the southern Adriondacks had been completely lumbered. Even more devastating to the forest's survival was the practice of leaving branches, tops, and non-useful trees where they fell so that the forest floor became covered with a loose latticework of branches, six to eight feet deep. This slash formed almost impenetrable areas of hazardous kindling.

The last decade of the nineteenth century and the first decade of the twentieth century were years of drought in the North. It was also a time when wood- and coal-fired railroads were first constructed through the Adirondacks. The dry slash, sparks from the trains, lightening, and carelessness resulted in fires that plagued the mountains and gave them their present character. Fed by the growth of small evergreens and the rubble on the forest floor, fires consumed whole mountainsides. The flames were so intense and the organic soils so shallow that all but the thin mineral soil burned.

This should be a message to hikers. Organic topsoil, being composed of dead vegetation, burns quite easily when dry. People can inadvertently start forest fires when they build a camp fire on ground they think is safe.

Great fires raged in the Adirondacks in 1880, 1889, 1903, 1908, and 1913. They are reported to have burned over a million acres of woodland. The largest fire, in 1903, burned 464,000 acres and was the tenth largest forest fire to have occurred in the U.S. and Canada in the period of 1825 to 1947. In the area covered by this guide, the 1903 fires burned part of Harrington Mountain and the valley of Stewart Creek, part of Moose Moun-

Garnet Lake and Mt. Blue from Crane Mountain's western trail

tain and an area south of Griffin, and a section in the towns of Thurman and Stony Creek north and northwest of Knowelhurst.

Charcoal-preserved remains of huge stumps can be found everywhere. They are less obvious in the valleys or wherever there is mineral soil and where the humus did not burn. In the valleys, the forests have recovered at a spectacular rate. Climax stands of oaks, maples, pines, and spruce tower over the narrow paths that are all that remain of the old logging roads.

On the drier slopes whole trunks can often be found, sometimes surrounded by bare rock, for on the steeper slopes recovery has been very slow. Mosses and lichens creep along the steep faces, beginning again the process of accumulating soil. Where there is no soil left to hold the precious water, spring is a time of raging floods and summer a time of dry rocky streams. On many of the peaks, there is no water at all in summer. The disruption of the soil's ability to retain moisture further slows the regrowth of mountain forests, and so these bare peaks may be open for many years to come.

With Crane rising over 3200 feet, more than 2000 feet above the valley to the east, and Mt Blue at over 2900 feet, rising 1500 feet above Garnet Lake, the list of open summits to scale is quite impressive. To the south, Baldhead at 2870 feet looms above the Stony Creek Valley, which lies little more than 2 miles from the summit. Hadley Mountain's summit is is over 2600 feet, making it almost 2000 feet above the nearby end of the Stony Creek Valley where it meets the Hudson. This list rounds out to a dozen open peaks, all with excellent views, a hiker's dream.

There are two problems. One is that only two of the peaks have trails to their summits. But if you have any bushwhacking experience at all, the trips to the summits along partially exposed ridges are remarkably easy. The other problem involves avoiding the private lands that lie in the valleys below the mountains, but, as this guide details, that can be done.

40 Crane, the Super Mountain
Drive, exploring geological origins

Before enjoying the climbs up Crane Mountain or the many views of Crane from nearby peaks, drive around this mammoth hunk of rock and get acquainted with its unbelievable mass, its sheer cliffs, and the way it dominates the countryside. Happily, there is a circular drive from which many of Crane's faces are visible.

As you leave the Northway at Warrensburg, Crane is the distant mountain visible to the northwest. Drive north from Warrensburg on either side of the Hudson, enjoying its river views. At the Glen, NY 28 crosses the Hudson. Just beyond the bridge, turn west, left, on Glen Creek Road. At 0.4 mile, a dirt road on the right leads to a small waterfall and swimming hole. In the next mile, the road and creek are in Forest Preserve land, both sheltered by a hemlock-filled gorge.

At 4.3 miles, turn south on South Johnsburg Road. As you approach Thurman, stop near the church to look at Crane's eastern cliffs. Turn west on Garnet Lake Road at Thurman. You pass the turnout for the Crane Mountain trail 1.25 miles from Thurman. The best view of Crane is 1.75 miles farther west where Little Pond, which is small and charmingly wooded with birches, is completely dominated by the rocky southern face of Crane. Three miles west, the road to Garnet Lake turns south. Your road turns north with openings where the cliffs seem to loom above the road.

There is a parking turnout and fishing access to Mill Creek 3 miles north. From here look across the cliffs of Huckleberry Mountain toward the western slopes of Crane. Less than 0.5 mile beyond, take a right turn, east on Hudson Street for views up the cleft valley of Paintbed Creek and the precipitous cliffs on Huckleberry. In 0.5 mile you cross that creek and pass a parking turnout. Continue northeast to intersect South Johnsburg Road to complete the circle.

You can easily add a drive along Goodman Road from Johnsburg west to Bakers Mills to the Crane Mountain circuit. There are a half dozen places along the road where the view to the southeast toward Crane is exceptional.

Local lore attributes the mountain's name to the cranes, blue heron, that nested in profusion around the pond part way up the mountain. However, recent research by F. B. Rosevear indicates that an early surveyor may have given his name to the mountain. There were possibly two surveyors named Crain and Crane whose work may have touched the mountain. Ebenezer Jessup's field notes of 1772 refer to a Joseph Crane, who laid out a "line of mile trees" 55 miles from the Hudson to the north line of the Totten and Crossfield Patent, which would have taken the line over Crane Mountain.

GEOLOGICAL ORIGINS

Crane Mountain is one of the places in the Adirondacks where the geologic origins of those mountains are vividly portrayed. The limestone and sandstone sediments that were deposited in the Grenville Sea, beginning about 2.3 billion years ago, were metamorphosed during a period of mountain building known as the Grenville Orogeny that began about 1.4 billion years ago and lasted for 400 million years. No one knows for certain the cause of these events; the possible collision of continental plates is one modern theory being considered.

Whatever the cause, the sediments were intruded by magma that cooled into coarsely crystalline rocks known as syenite, gabbro, and granite. The entire mass lay several miles beneath the surface of the earth, where heat and pressure metamorphosed the sediments into quartzite, marble, and skarn, and the igneous intrusions into syenite gneiss, granite gneiss, and metagabbro. These rocks were folded and warped by metamorphism to produce banding that looks like multicolored taffy.

Only the rocks persist from this Precambrian era, for the mountains themselves are much newer. Another period of slow uplift began 400 million years ago. In addition, mountain building in New England created faults in the Adirondacks along which later erosion cut the valleys and helped the ice shape the mountains to their modern form.

It is the Grenville Orogeny that is vividly portrayed on Crane Mountain. Ingvar Isachsen, geologist with the New York State Museum, has described the mountain as a four-decker, bent sandwich with a layer of marble near the base of the mountain, above this a layer of resistant granite gneiss known as charnokite, above this a layer of marble and other easily eroded rocks at the level of the bench line where the pond lies, and finally, on top, another layer of charnokite.

Looking at the mountain from the southeast, you can clearly see the top three layers.

41 Crane Mountain

Marked trail, hiking, camping, fishing, berrying

There are 5.2 miles of marked trails on Crane Mountain and a 1300-foot climb to its summit. With unmarked paths, bushwhacks, and much to explore, it is worth several trips. To make it easier for you to plan a variety of expeditions, the description of trails and paths has been broken down into segments so you can choose ways to combine them.

Ladders on Crane Mountain

View Northwest from Crane with Huckleberry's cliffs

THE TRAILHEAD

Drive west from Thurman on the Garnet Lake Road for 1.5 miles and turn right onto a dirt road with a sign indicating the trailhead. Continue nearly 2 miles on the dirt road, but use caution driving. The road climbs fairly steeply, and its washes make it quite difficult at some times of the year. At a fork near the end of the road, keep right. The way left leads to a house on Putnam Farm Road, which used to be part of the trail system on Crane. The new trailhead and a short section of new trail circle avoid the house.

THE WESTERN TRAIL TO CRANE MOUNTAIN POND
1.9 miles one way, 1¼ hours, 900-foot vertical rise

From the west of the parking area, a narrow footpath leads 0.4 mile to intersect the old Putnam Farm Road. Valley residents use this road to ski across the base of the mountain, but the western end is privately owned. The western trail leaves the road, 1 mile west of the trailhead.

Immediately north of the road, the trail crosses Putnam Brook in a most dramatic fashion. Do stop and investigate the natural stone bridge. Upstream the brook disappears into the ground, emerging just downstream from the bridge from a small cave leached from the soft marble layer at the base of the mountain.

The 0.9-mile climb up the mountain to the outlet of the pond, 900 feet above, is obviously steep. Very quickly, enough elevation is gained so that views to the south begin. The way is marked and presents but one problem on the ascent. As you approach the large, open rock field, go left and carefully cross the outlet of the pond. If you are descending this way, when you first cross the outlet, stay close to it to find the continuing route. Hikers have been misled by walking out onto the sheer, rounded, granite face away from the trail. The face of the mountain is deceptively steep.

The trail continues through the woods west of the stream and reaches the pond at its outlet.

THE NORTHWESTERN SHOULDER OF CRANE MOUNTAIN
Unmarked footpath

Immediately west of the outlet of the pond, an unmarked footpath leads uphill. (Another path follows the western shore, 50 to 100 feet back from it, leading to several camping spots.) The path to the western summit connects a series of open rock patches winding up the narrow ridge line. You should have no problem following it, except where a pair of glacial erratics seems to bar the way. Head left here toward the edge of the cliffs. A breathtaking scramble leads on toward the summit, 220 feet above the pond, and farther west and down to a vantage with a superb northwestern view. This point is about 0.75 mile from the pond.

The southerly views lead from Number Four Mountain on the east, to Baldhead and Moose, Bearpen Ridge, Mt. Blue, Ross and Armstrong, and around to Eleventh Mountain on the northwest. Beyond the sheer drop to Putnam Farm Road lies Garnet Lake. To the west of the cliffs of Huckleberry, you see Gore Mountain.

Notice how hollow your footsteps sound crossing the open rock. The echoes are from exfoliation sheaves, slabs of rock that scale off from the mountain as internal pressures have been released or as freezing water has broken them loose. Between the rock patches are pockets of moss and lichens, covered with a carpet of blueberries, graced in June with pink lady slipper orchids. Clumps of balsam and spruce are a backdrop to gardens of sculptured rock and boulders carefully placed by the last glacier.

THE POND AND THE NORTH KNOB
From the outlet, the marked trail heads east around the pond. Rock shelves substitute for beaches at the best places to swim. The pond has been stocked

Crane Mountain Pond

with trout and no live bait can be used. A ten-minute walk brings you to the southeast corner where a red-marked trail continues along the bench line to interrersect the eastern trail in 0.4 mile.

The summit trail turns north and when last walked, the next intersection was under two feet of water—the beaver dam at the outlet was responsible. Even without high water, this is a wet place. Past the summit trail, you will see a faint footpath angling northwest up the north knob. The way is so open and so many have walked this way, it is hardly a bushwhack. Just climb up the ledge to the best vantage, a view over the lake to the tops of distant mountains.

THE SUMMIT FROM THE POND
1 mile from the outlet of the pond, 40 minutes, 600-foot vertical rise

From the wet intersection at the northeast corner of the pond, a trail climbs southwest 600 feet in 0.6 mile to the summit. Some of the best views are not right at the top, but from a rock outcrop west of the summit. There is a footpath, unmarked, that leads 200 feet to these rocks. It is a right, south, fork from the trail 0.2 mile below the summit. From the overlook, Crane Mountain Pond appears below as a gem in a setting of rugged hills and rocks. To the northwest, Snowy Mountain, behind Indian Lake, is clearly visible and on a really clear day, some of the High Peaks can be identified.

You may have trouble finding the fork; others have. If you miss it, do return from the summit to look for it. On the climb from the pond, begin to look for it as the trees become smaller and open rock patches appear.

From the outcrop, return to the trail and continue east across the top of the cliffs to the tower, which is closed. This tower, the second built on Crane, replaced one built in 1904, making it among the first to warn against that decade's numerous fires.

Views to the south are possible all along the top of the cliffs. Notice especially Mt. Blue to the southwest behind Garnet Lake and Baldhead, Moose, and Hadley mountains to the south.

THE EASTERN TRAIL
1.9 miles one way, 1¼ hours, 1300-foot vertical rise.

Because the western approach offers views so quickly, it always seems best to circle the mountain in a clockwise fashion, returning from the summit via the eastern trail. To find the red-marked trail at the summit, walk east of the tower. Ladders and cables assist the steep climb down a small rubble-filled draw in the rock face. The trail swings to the west, below the upper cliffs and continues descending to the intersection with the bench trail to the lake. The bench trail, a right fork, descends nearly 200 feet more to the level of the lake. The 0.4-mile descent so far will take as much as thirty minutes.

To continue the descent to the parking area, take the right fork, which descends steeply at first through a beautiful canopy of white and yellow birch.

If you are using this trail to climb Crane, you will find its beginning at the north end of the parking area. It heads north, gently at first, then very steeply. As the trees become smaller, after a forty-minute climb, you will find ledges with views and an excuse to stop and rest. At the second outcrop, the continuing route may still be poorly marked, though from partway across the open rock a trail marker should be visible on a tree a little east of north.

Beyond, the trail forks. The summit trail turns east beneath the cliffs. A ladder assists your climb over a short ledge. You continue east, then briefly southeast, to reach the point where a scramble up the remaining 100-foot cliff is possible. The ladders seem precarious. You could probably make the ascent using handholds beside the ladder. At the top, walk 100 yards west to the summit.

Giant boulders beneath Huckleberry Mountain

42 The Paint Mine

Footpath, hiking, exploring

The deep cleft north of Crane Mountain is a long valley separating Crane and Huckleberry. Not only is there something new and exciting there to explore, but thanks to Hamilton County historian Ted Aber, there are new details to fill in its history.

According to local lore, paint from the mine in the cleft was used as early as 1850 on some houses in Johnsburg. The particular blend of aluminum and iron oxides found there made an indestructible paint. D. M. Haley rediscovered the mine in 1893 and bored down 70 feet, finding no bottom to the ore. In the spring of 1894 he built a 60- by 40-foot factory to produce paint from the ore. The building was destroyed by fire after only two seasons. Early in 1898, Haley was living in a house at the foot of Crane, planning to rebuild the plant.

On February 28, 1898, heavy rain loosened the snow above and early the next day an avalanche of snow, ice, and rock fell into the valley. The mass, deflected by a large boulder, struck only a part of the building, destroying it, but the occupants were spared. Undaunted, Haley continued the mining operation for a few more years, but within the year he had located his plant in Saratoga.

Not only can you find the foundations of the mine and some of the pits in the cleft, but now you can also marvel at the boulders plucked from the cliffs of Huckleberry by glaciers and more recent avalanches.

A state parking area is on the south side of Hudson Street, just east of Painted Brook. West of the brook, a dirt road, Paintbed Road, heads southwest, uphill, away from the brook. While this is the only road shown on the North Creek Quadrangle, there is a left fork beyond the top of the initial stiff climb at about 150°. This branch soon reaches a steep, rocky stretch probably impassable by cars, then also forks.

The left branch soon reaches a triple fork, the rightmost being the road to Snowshoe Pond. To the left a path almost concealed by scrubby growth leads through an open grassy area again at about 150° and becomes an old tote road. This is the way to the Paint Mine.

The route is downhill, through brambles, with through-the-trees views of the cliffs on Huckleberry. Yellow blazes denote the end of private land within a ten-minute walk from the jeep road. You cross a tributary of Paintbed Brook. The path angles back close to, but high above, that brook. At a second brook crossing, the cliffs, closer now, are clearly visible. A third brook has a brush-covered, decrepit bridge. Dull reddish blazes (paint from the mine?) increase in number.

After a thirty-five-minute walk, the valley has narrowed and the trail is quite close to Huckleberry. You may not even notice the beginning of the walk's surprise. Near the crossing of Paintbed Brook, here as small as the tributaries you have crossed, the red-marked old road continues straight up the right side of the draw. The spot is near a complex of boulders with a protected cavelike opening among the enormous rocks. You will want to go left toward the cliffs on the newly cut path, already more obvious than the roadway. Someone has devised a new route that will take you beneath these gigantic boulders, some as tall 'as three or four stories.

Within a 0.25 mile, the path levels out on the high saddle. As it does, it rejoins the old road, a place now hard to find. Now it is time to start looking for the first hole in the ground to the right of the path. Five minutes later, as the valley is becoming broad, keep looking to your right. First you will spot the chimney of one of the factory buildings, near it a giant erratic—the one that deflected the avalanche and prevented it from destroying all of the house. Foundations of the first factory are nearby, with birches and other trees nearly two feet in diameter growing from it.

The path continues, passing a small marsh. Later it joins Crystal Brook and descends to the east, to posted land. Your trip to the paint mine would be pleasant as a ski or snowshoe trip in winter when the boulders would be all the more visible. The hike to the mine takes an hour and a quarter, one way.

43 Crane Mountain's North Face
Bushwhack

If you have tried all the other approaches to the mountain and are an experienced bushwhacker, this route is for you. It is the only route on Crane that is safe for snowshoes in winter—the southern faces are all too often sheets of ice.

Walk to the paint mine on the path described above and continue through the saddle. Your plan will be to intercept Crystal Brook, which drains the east side of the valley, and follow it nearly to its source in a spring not far below the level of Crane Mountain Pond. Since you would have to detour to the east to pick it up if you followed the continuing path, start your bushwhack just beyond the marsh. Hugging Crane Mountain, strike a course to the southeast, climbing where it is not too steep until you reach the brook. There is rarely any flowing water in the brook, just a series of cascades of emerald, moss-covered rocks or, in winter, ranks of frozen icicles.

Follow the stream uphill. The going is rough and climbing prematurely away from the draw will only lead to areas that are too steep or to a knob away from the main part of the mountain. Where the stream levels out and the valley seems extremely brushy, climb the west bank, going up no more than 100 feet from the brook. You will cross another tiny brook, flowing from the west. You are west of the place where Crystal Brook itself emerges as a seep from a headwall below the level of the pond.

As you angle up and away from the brook, the change from the deep, damp woods near the stream is most dramatic. Within a short distance, the results of past fires become obvious. There are patches of bare rock, surrounded by a thin cover of dry mosses and lichens that crunch underfoot. Walk from one open patch to the next, climbing gradually on a course a little west of south until you see the pond. This route avoids the swampy area at the north of the pond.

On the return this way, follow the path along the west shore and continue level for 200 yards, then drop gradually down to the level of the brook. The trip from the parking area takes nearly two and a half hours, the descent just slightly less.

Chimney from the paint mine

44 Huckleberry Mountain
Bushwhack

Huckleberry is a smaller copy of Crane, less complex, but encased with cliffs along its mile-and-a-half southern and southwestern face. A bush-whack to its summit involves an 1100-foot climb, 200 feet more than the climb to Crane's summit via its south face trails. Huckleberry's views are not as spectacular as Crane's, but its summit ridge is one of the most delight-ful places you can walk. Only the ridge line and cliffs are state land; all accesses are private but unposted. Permission to climb may be required.

The easiest approach starts from the same parking area near Paintbed Brook on Hudson Street south of Johnsburg as in section 42. Walk along the road on the east side of the brook. Within 200 yards, you enter a clear-ing with the western end of Huckleberry right above you. The road bears east out of the clearing. Follow it, taking the upper road where it forks. Just beyond the fork, head uphill through a tangle of logged tops and bram-bles. The mess is brief enough.

You will be walking almost due south, climbing fairly steadily. The west-ern end of the mountain makes a long arc to the north. Following this ridge line gives the least steep ascent and keeps you closest to the edge for views. Changes in tree cover mark your elevation. Beyond the logged area, stands of hemlock cling to the steep slopes. Red pine with an occa-sional striped maple or oak alert you to the coming views. Your first one is west from the edge of an open patch in a level area, just below the 2000-foot line. Even getting to this point requires careful choices on the routes around ledges.

Uphill, the way remains steep, but as the views increase, you hardly no-tice the climb. Crane appears so close, and you can see beyond it to a corner of Garnet Lake with Mt. Blue behind. The more western ledges look northwest to Gore Mountain. The only disappointment is the lack of any openings to the north where the slopes all appear to be heavily wooded.

As wonderful as the views into the cleft and beyond is the walk across the ridge. For the better part of a mile you can easily navigate between outcrops and cliff tops, sometimes ducking back in to the trees, a spectacu-lar open forest of red pine. The cushion of needles underfoot supports sweet-

Huckleberry Mountain cliffs

fern shrub. Bearberry and three-leaf cinquefoil cling to the sloping top of the escarpment.

The ascent described takes an hour and a half, the descent takes an hour and a quarter. Allow more for following the cliff tops to the east or continuing to climb the eastern knob, which punctuates the escarpment.

45 Garnet Lake
Picnic spots, campsites, fishing

Garnet Lake is quite typical of the area's lakes in that it was enlarged by a dam. Others are Lens, Harrisburg, Middle Flow, and Livingstone. Garnet Lake shows on the 1898 USGS map, reprinted in 1923, as a lake of less than half the area of the present one. It was then named Mill Creek Pond and had huge swamps stretching more than a mile along the inlet on the south. In the 1930s, Ralph Maxim, who owned a considerable amount of the surrounding land as well as much of the lakeshore, arranged to dam the lake, raising its level exactly five feet. This small amount more than doubled the lake's size. Although Mr. Maxim had logged much of the land before it was flooded, the southern two-thirds of the present lake is peppered with stumps, many above water and more than a few lying just below the surface, waiting to snag the unwary canoe.

Much of Garnet Lake is covered with water lilies and pond weeds as well as the ubiquitous stumps, but it is not the surface that gives the lake its dramatic character. Looming above it on the west is a range of dramatic mountains. Buck Hill rises to 2160 feet, 700 feet above the surface of the lake. Farther south, Ross Mountain, 2625 feet, has a rugged outcrop of bare rock below its summit. Capping the chain on the south, Mt. Blue rises so precipitously and imposingly on the west side of the lake that it overhwelms it. Its summit of 2925 feet elevation rises almost 1500 feet above the lake in a distance of less than ¾ mile from shore.

Along the eastern shore there is a section of state land, beginning less than 0.5 mile from the outlet, with several picnic spots, sandy beaches with good places to swim, and small parking turnouts.

No camping is allowed at these sites, but there are a number of good camping places on the southwestern shore and around the peninsula that juts out from the eastern shore. The majority are most easily approached from the water. All are a short canoe ride from the picnic spots, which double as good canoe-launching sites.

46 Mud Pond

Canoeing, fishing, skiing, snowshoeing

A dirt road heads south, 2.1 miles east of the entrance to Garnet Lake on the Garnet Lake Road and 1.1 miles west of Little Pond. The road is gated at a private inholding 0.9 miles south. A sign at the turn indicates this as a snowmobile trail with Mud Pond 0.8 miles distant, Round Pond 1.6 miles away. However, posted signs at the gate indicate that a through trip on the trail to Round Pond is not possible.

On the way to Round Pond

In winter you will want to ski to Mud Pond and continue on over frozen meadows to Round Pond. In summer you can either walk the road or drive with a canoe and make the short carry to the pond.

The road climbs 200 feet in 0.8 mile to the top of a rise where there is a turnaround on the left with room to park. Do not drive farther as there is no place to turn around by the gate. A path leads south from here 200 yards to Mud Pond and the path's width permits easy carrying. You could camp near the end of the path.

In the past this small pond was the archetypal dying lake, encircled by a true quaking bog. Beaver have raised the level over a foot with a mud dam that is at least 200 feet long across the outlet to the west, toward Round Pond. Most of the bog plants have been flooded, though a thick stand of common cattails remains on the south shore.

47 Round Pond from the Northeast
Skiing, showshoeing, canoeing

Hikers heading for Round Pond should use the trail from Garnet Lake, section 48. Currently reaching Round Pond by canoe is a challenge: beaver have constructed a series of small dams, as many as twenty-five in all. (You do lose count.) With patience, an hour to spare, and the strength to lift a canoe over these low dams and pull it through several narrow channels where alders squeeze in from the sides, you could canoe the 0.7 mile outlet. That distance is greater if one counts all the meanders through the swamp. Round Pond is only three feet lower than Mud Pond.

Most of the small lakes and ponds to explore in the area covered by this guide are shallow, muddy, or boggy. It is a real treat to find one with clear water, sandy beaches, and great variety and beauty. Round Pond, which is far from round, is one of the gems in the area: a crystal sheet of water surrounded by spruce- and hemlock-covered shores dotted with white birch. Bearpen Peak dominates the southwestern end and the conical form of Wolf Pond Mountain surmounts the southeastern shores. You will find campsites on the small peninsula that lies west of the inlet. There is a sandy beach farther west.

The best way to use this approach to the pond is on skis in winter. You can easily ski to Mud Pond and follow the frozen marshes southwest to explore Round Pond. The round trip gives you 4 miles of good skiing.

Lixard Pond

48 Round Pond from Garnet Lake

Marked snowmobile trail, hiking, fishing, snowshoeing
2 miles one way, 1½ hours, 600-foot vertical rise

A very good, open route, marked as a snowmobile trail, leads to Round Pond from Garnet Lake. There is little evidence that this route is used in summer, though it's a fine short hike. No paths around the shore appear to emanate from the marsh at the end of the trail.

The trailhead is on the east shore of Garnet Lake, 0.8 mile south of the dam and just 100 feet north of a barrier on the road that continues on private land. The trail heads up a grade and follows an old log road through stands of white and yellow birch and hemlock. In fifteen minutes you see boulders and ledges on the hill to the northeast. You continue winding along relatively level ground, generally southeast below the hillside.

The trail crosses a brook at an acute angle and a five-minute walk later begins to climb after crossing a second small brook. The trail angles to the south and continues climbing through a draw. The route is out to the western edge of the hill, so that after an hour of walking there are glimpses of Garnet Lake, if the leaves are off the trees.

The trail swings southeast again, across a level, and with one more sharp rise crosses the height-of-land in a draw 200 feet above the pond. On the way down to the pond, the trail winds past a group of glacial erratics arranged around a small grotto.

While the walk is very pleasant, I will always remember it for the barred owl who guarded the approach to the first slopes. Perched not twenty feet above the ground, he stared at us with his brilliant orange eyes and mewed menacingly like a perturbed cat.

49 Lixard Pond

Marked snowmobile trail, hiking, camping, skiing, fishing
One way trip is 1 mile by canoe plus 1-mile walk, 1 hour,
200-foot vertical rise

Lixard Pond is called "Lizard" by everyone, and that was probably its original name. The corruption may have come from an early mapmaker's misspelling predating even the 1898 USGS.

The pond is very long—over 0.5 mile—and narrow, lying nearly east-west and below the southern face of Mt. Blue. The route to the pond is along a marked path that follows both an old road and an established fishermen's path. Lixard Pond has been reclaimed and stocked with trout and provides some pretty good fishing.

The trailhead is directly across Garnet Lake and west of the peninsula on the eastern shore, a handsome 1-mile-long paddle from the parking area on the east shore of Garnet Lake. If you are a fisherman, you might try your luck in Garnet Lake on the way to the trailhead, where there is a good campsite.

The trailhead lies at the foot of the valley between Mt. Blue and Gillingham Knoll. The trail heads uphill for 200 yards to cross an unmarked old roadway. The way east is an abandoned snowmobile trail to Madison Creek Flow, currently difficult to follow and full of blowdowns. The way west follows the western shore of Garnet Lake back to private land. This old road can be used as an approach to the Lixard Pond Trail, but only with permission from the landowner at the end of the west shore road.

The trail curves from south to southeast through the draw, on high ground. It picks up the company of a very small stream partway to the

View from Mt. Blue

pond. As the trail approaches the pond, the terrain levels out. You continue beside the marshes that fill the pond's eastern end. You can extend the gentle climb by walking west along the shore, enjoying views of open rock and the exposed face of Mt. Blue. After you cross the pond's principal outlet, a very tiny stream most of the year, the trail winds through hemlock groves to a lean-to near the western end. There are several good camping spots along the way, good for part of an interior camping trip or day walks toward Baldwin Springs or up Mt. Blue.

In winter, it is fun to ski across Garnet Lake and up to the pond. With snowshoes you are prepared for a winter ascent of Mt. Blue.

50 Mt. Blue
Bushwhack, hiking or on snowshoes

You can extend the canoe ride and walk to Lixard Pond to a full-day outing with this bushwhack, which is extraordinarily easy to navigate. Mt. Blue so dominates Garnet Lake that it would seem the climb might be formidable. However, the mountain is easily conquered and because the bushwhack does not require great experience, this is the most delightful of all those leading to open peaks.

The views are spectacular, really superlative. The view northeast to Crane shows the broadest range of that mountain's two-and-a-half-mile sweep of cliffs and bare rock, which rise more than a thousand feet from the valley.

To the south and southeast, Lixard Pond and the flows beyond guide the viewer toward Bearpen Peak and Baldhead and Moose mountains. In the far south, the depressions of the East Stony Creek Valley and the Lens Lake Valley are both delineated. You can pick out Georgia and Harrington mountains on the west, and there is an excellent view of New Lake Mountain, with Wilcox Mountain behind in the southwest. You can even see a corner of Indian Pond and part of Madison Creek Flow. With views like these, the only problem is to be sure and pick a clear day for the ascent.

A savage fire, which started in September of 1908 after a summer of drought, burned the entire southeastern side of the mountain. Patches all over the top half of this side of the mountain remain treeless, a boon to bushwhacking and viewing, and any ascent should take advantage of them.

The recommended route is northwest, along the long ridge, starting from a point on the Lixard Pond Trail where the swamps in the pond's valley first become visible from the trail. Using this ridge, you can find patches of open rock after climbing less than a third of the remaining 1200 feet to the summit. Even from the vantage of the lower rock outcrops, the views are enticing, and after two-thirds of the climb, the views are extraordinary.

About two-thirds of the way up, angle a little to the north, just for the views. There is a cleft near the summit where you will have to search about for ways over the ledges. The summit itself is wooded, but ledges below the summit permit views through 270 degrees.

You will need a compass only for the bottom third of the walk. A word of caution: take plenty of liquids; this can be a very hot and dry walk.

The southwest faces of Mt. Blue are sufficiently open so that it would not be difficult to bushwhack to a tiny teardrop-shaped pond concealed in the high valley west of the summit. That pond is almost 700 feet below the summit, so it adds considerably to the bushwhack. A circular walk south along the teardrop's outlet to the Lixard Pond Trail is possible but does not take the best advantage of open rock.

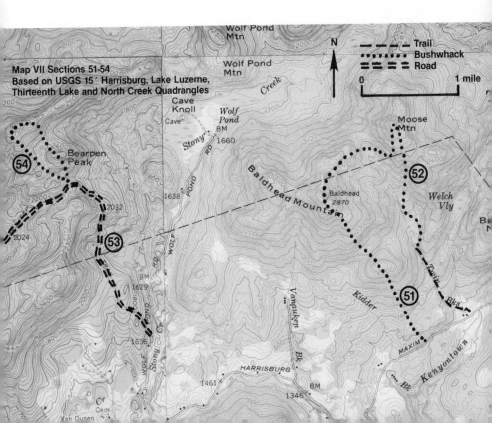

Balancing rock on Baldhead Mountain

51 Baldhead Mountain
Bushwhack

Baldhead is another in the string of open peaks and lies almost due south of Crane. The top third of the mountain has bare patches all around the southern face from west to east. These make the climbing fairly easy and permit many distant views even before the summit is reached. With the open peak and the 1500-foot climb, the bushwhack rivals the excitement of some of the High Peaks.

As with many of the open peaks, the main problem in climbing the mountain is finding good access on state land. The best is from Tucker Road. Drive 4.6 miles north of Stony Creek on the Harrisburg Road, turn right onto Tucker for 1 mile, and park on the right side at a small turnout at the height-of-land. A course of due magnetic north will start you toward the mountain. This route takes you through open woods, crossing two small ravines at right angles. Beyond a small brook, notice the marvelously tall, straight maples. In thirty minutes you reach a small knob. After a very short descent, you start uphill again.

Because the private land to the north has been logged and the boundary recently painted, continue north until you reach it, then angle to the west to follow it. It makes a very easy guide for this part of the climb. Open patches from a 1940s fire make the way easy. A second, larger knob lies to the west of this course, but already you have some views. It takes about an hour for the 700-foot, 1-mile-long climb to this point.

Beyond the knob, pick a course to the northwest. You descend a 200-foot deep ravine, after which the climbing is noticeably steeper. Within half an hour you encounter lots of open patches with memorable views back over the valley of the Hudson to mountains near Lake George. The open patches are lovely rock gardens of moss and lichen with mountain ash. A slight break in the climb is followed by a steep thrust. More open patches with woods between line the route, making it easy to choose your course toward the summit. You climb 900 feet from the draw in 0.7 mile, a steep bushwhack that can take over an hour.

A stone fire ring and red arrows greet you as you reach the summit ridge. The arrows point northwest across the ridge to a favorite perch overlooking Moose Mountain, the valley between the peaks, and Mt. Blue and Crane Mountain. There is a 1942 benchmark at the summit and north of it an intriguing balancing rock. The trip to the summit, over 2 miles with nearly a 1700-foot climb, takes between two and two and a half hours. You can reverse course for a fairly easy return trip.

52 Moose Mountain
Bushwhack

There are two routes to Moose Mountain. The most direct begins with a walk up the private road following Twin Brooks. That road is a right turn from Tucker Road, 1.6 miles northeast of the Harrisburg Road. Permission is given to walk this road to the property of Dominick Di Lorenzo and cross his private lands. The tract surrounding the marsh at the end of the road has recently been acquired by the state, significantly improving public access. You must, however, leave a car on Tucker Road, as no permission to drive this road has been given, and in fact it is suitable only for ATVs.

The road climbs to a bridge over Twin Brooks in less than ¼ mile and then forks left to continue the uphill course. The route is high above the brook in a lovely hemlock-filled gorge. A mile up the valley, past the Di Lorenzo cabin, the road reaches a long beaver marsh and circles it on the east. Leave the roadway, almost at its end, and take a couse of just east of magnetic north. Several steep ravines converge toward the marsh area. Pick a course on high ground above the deepest parts of the ravines. Your route will take a slight arc to the east then back toward magnetic north as it approaches the summit. It is a stiff 1100-foot climb in 1¼ miles from the end of the road, with the compensating factor that open patches are reached after a little more than half the ascent. The climb will take two to two and a half hours.

A more exciting way to enjoy Moose Mountain is an extension of the climb up Baldhead. This super circuit of both peaks involves a 6-mile trek, mostly bushwhacking and a climb of 2200 feet. It takes at least seven and a half hours.

From the summit of Baldhead, section 51, walk all the way west until the mountain starts to fall away. Then descend to the northwest. Your object will be to use high ground of the arc to the north that connects the two mountains. This route minimizes the climbing, but it does involve some steep places. As it is, you descend 540 feet from Baldhead, only to climb almost that high to the summit of Moose.

Stay on high ground close to the western edge of the arc as you curve around, descending where it seems logical, enjoying the birch-covered slopes. There are openings with views back up to Baldhead and the balancing rock. It takes forty minutes to reach the low point. (An old horse trail crosses the col at this point, coming from the west side of the marsh at the end of the road beside Twin Brooks. This trail circles around Baldhead and ultimately reaches Wolf Pond Road. It could be used as an alternate approach to either mountain.)

From the low point, walk almost east, climbing where it seems easy, to avoid the steepest slopes. After ¼ mile on this course, swing back to northwest toward the summit. You reach spectacular views well before you reach the summit.

The climb from the col takes about forty minutes. Again, the walk approaching the summit is a delightful trek from ledge to ledge, with views of Wolf Pond, Wolf Pond Mountain, Bearpen, and Baldhead to Hadley. You see all of Crane and, to the west of it, the distant High Peaks. The summit is wooded, but a few feet below it, you can circle around and find vantages in all directions.

To descend from Moose, pick a course toward magnetic south from the summit, following open ledges. Note a small cleft to your right. Do not try to follow it, but stay to the left of it. You run out of open patches after twenty to twenty-five minutes. Continue your course, keeping away from and northeast of the ravine that forms to your right. When the way seems a bit less steep, an hour and ten minutes from the top, after 1¼ miles and an 1100-foot descent (an altimeter certainly helps here), you should come out in an area that has been recently logged. Look for the logging road that hugs the east side of the beaver swamp. It will take you all the way to Tucker Road.

Even walking the road is pleasant, for it follows the hemlock-covered gorge of the eastern branch of Twin Brooks. A thirty-minute walk takes you down to a bridge over the brook, and a right fork takes you to the road—a fifteen-minute walk and a little over ½ mile east of your car if your trek was part of the Baldhead circuit.

Over the Mountain, Thurman and Stony Creek

THE TOWN OF Thurman was settled shortly after the Revolution by Scots families who migrated north along the Hudson. Their farms were mostly in the valleys and close to the river. Only a few rugged individuals ventured into the western parts of the town.

The Town of Stony Creek was originally part of the Town of Thurman. In the early nineteenth century, it was a mountainous wilderness, only sparsely settled, with a few farms and grist mills. The abundant forests were the area's principal resource. The availability of water, both to power the sawmills and to float the logs to market, helped the lumbering operations flourish. Potash was produced by burning the abundant supplies of wood.

In the second half of that century, there were many industries that made wood products. Tanning became an important source of income, and the huge stands of hemlock were cut for their bark. In those days, Stony Creek was a community nearly three times as large as it was to be in the 1960s. In the late 1800s, hardwood trees were cut; much of what remained was cut for pulp. Lumbering for pulp persisted into the 1920s, and there were two sawmills in Knowelhurst, which is the junction of Wolf Pond and Harrisburg Roads. There were other sawmills in the area, and there is some harvesting of pulpwood today.

Following the years of heavy lumbering came the years of fires, a fatal blow to the forest's productivity. Even the flow of water was affected. People left to find an easier time elsewhere. Unlike some of the villages that disappeared altogether, Stony Creek remained, with its residents serving hunters and other outdoor people who love the surrounding mountains.

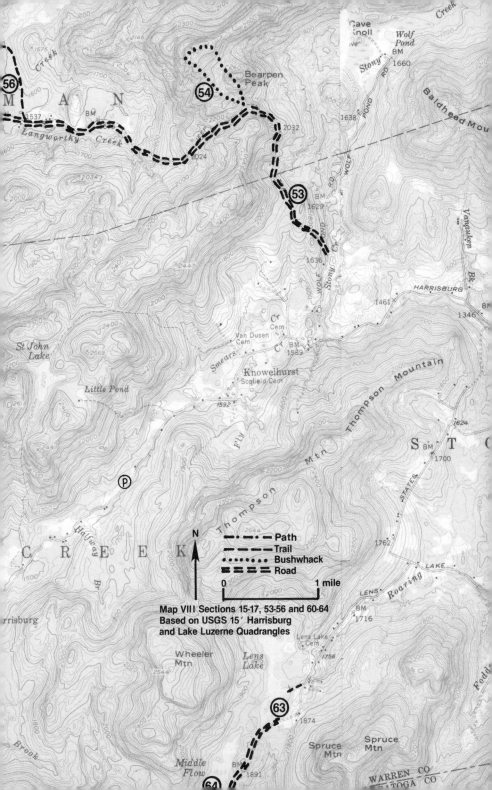

Path
Trail
Bushwhack
Road

0   1 mile

Map VIII Sections 15-17, 53-56 and 60-64
Based on USGS 15' Harrisburg
and Lake Luzerne Quadrangles

53 West Stony Creek Road
Drive to Baldwin Springs

The interior mountains and valleys are the concern of this guide. Of the several ways to reach them, the most fascinating is the West Stony Creek Road. The drive to Baldwin Springs is not only a trip into the past, it is a real adventure. Spring repairs and continuing work make this road suitable, most of the summer, for ordinary vehicles. Use caution and watch the rocks. At other times, walking or skiing the road is delightful. It leads to many of the old roads described in the first half of the guide, a number of opportunities for ski-touring or hiking.

The "trip over the mountain" is a relative newcomer; records indicate it is no more than a century old. Even when the interior was settled, the area around Baldwin Springs was never far removed from the remote wilderness found there today.

Head north then west from the center of Stony Creek on the Harrisburg Road for 5.7 miles, and make a right turn on Wolf Pond Road. At 1 mile (the following mileages are all given from Harrisburg Road), turn west onto an unmarked left fork. This is the West Stony Creek Road, which winds in and out of Forest Preserve land as it climbs 600 feet up a shoulder of Bearpen Mountain. New work along the road has created a number of turnouts on state land. Note the one at the crest of the hill, 3 miles from Harrisburg Road.

The road descends 800 feet to Baldwin Springs, the steepest part in the first 2 miles before a bridge over a tributary of Langworthy Creek. At 5.7 miles you pass the driveway to the remaining building of the Barber place. Opposite is a small pond with a picnic table. This site of the Barber place is now state-owned, and it is a lovely place to stop and enjoy the view northeast to Bearpen Peak and Long Tom Ridge.

The parking turnout for the snowmobile trail to Stone Dam follows at 5.9 miles. You probably will not even notice the abandoned trail to Harrisburg that was built to avoid private land south of Baldwin Springs. It heads south at 6.4 miles and is unusable. In another 0.2 mile you cross Madison Creek and at 7.6 miles reach the Hub at Baldwin Springs. A left, south, turn 0.3 mile later leads to the snowmobile bridge over the East Stony Creek. The road ends at Fullers and the Dog and Pup Club at 8.3 miles.

You might want to stop and enjoy the rich woods on the small hill west

Tall tamarack near Baldwin Springs

of Madison Creek, where maidenhair and Goldie's fern abound. The transition from the hemlock woods of the gorge just below Bearpen Peak, to the conifer stands on the rich glacial soil in the valley, to the nearly treeless barrens near Baldwin Springs gives unusual variety to the drive. In winter the road makes a challenging ski trip. With distances this great, it is difficult to continue on most of the following interior trips in winter.

There never were more than a handful of houses along the remote road. It was as easy to reach the distant settlements from NY 8 and the Oregon Trail. The Randall Combs, Glassbroook, and Harvey Combs farms have long been deserted. Randall Combs' place became Gy-ba-Jk, the estate of Gutherie Barber.

54 Bearpen Peak and Long Tom Ridge
Bushwhack

A bushwhack to the cliffs and exposed rocky areas on the mountain northwest of the West Stony Creek Road is surprisingly easy, especially considering the fabulous views that will reward you. The USGS names a southwestern peak on this long mountain as Bearpen, but local residents refer to the whole ridge as Long Tom.

The bushwhack up Bearpen begins from parking turnouts at the height-of-land, 3 miles from Harrisburg Road. A path has developed from the northern turnout. It climbs a small knob and continues to Bearpen Peak. To avoid the knob, walk back east about 100 yards, then enter the woods on the north side of the road. Circle east, then north, around the small knob that lies northwest of the parking spots.

This will take you, in just a few minutes, to a small creek that drops steeply to the east through a little gorge. Cross the creek just west of the head of the gorge, and climb almost due north up the hill. In a remarkably short distance, you reach stretches of open rock with rudimentary paths between them. Within ten minutes walking time there are views toward the south and southeast. The open rock continues to the summit of Bearpen Peak. From the top of the cliffs on the peak you look down Wolf Pond Valley toward Stony Creek, with Hadley in the distance. This 350-foot climb covers ⅓ mile.

To continue to Long Tom Ridge, descend from the peak to the north-northwest, passing east of a wet woods. Then climb directly up the nearly mile-and-a-half-long ridge that runs from southwest to northeast. This course

View from Long Tom Ridge

will take you to a point about one-quarter of the way north from the southern end.

There are no large, exposed cliffs or rocky areas on the northwest side of the ridge, though there are a couple of openings in the trees across to Mt. Blue. At the far northern end of the ridge, there is a large overlook just below the top of the ridge looking south. The best views of all are from the southwestern end of the ridge, which is faced with two ranks of high cliffs.

Walk southwest along the ridge from open area to open area, until you reach the cliff tops. Even the places between the edges of the open rock patches pose no problems because they are filled with choke cherries instead of brambles. The views from the top of the highest cliff at the southwestern end of the ridge are spectacular. Snowy Mountain, behind Indian Lake, is visible. You can distinguish the valley of the East Branch of the Sacandaga and name a few of the mountains north of it. Georgia Mountain lies to the west. Madison Creek flows through the valley west of Long Tom Ridge. The site of the Barber place spreads out, south of west, below.

Strung out to the south is the range of hills that line the northwest of Harrisburg Valley, and beyond them you can see Hadley Mountain.

The descent could be a return over Bearpen Peak, but you may find it easier to head east-southeast toward the swampy area you passed on the way up. This time you walk on the south side of it. The swamp drains through a draw pointed southeast into the stream you crossed just after you left the road. On this descent, you cross the heads of several draws heading south or southwest. Avoid them and keep going southeast until you find the stream heading east. Take a route along it to the recognizable gorge, then walk south to the road.

A short loop to the southwestern edge of the ridge from the height-of-land on West Stony Creek Road requires three hours. Adding a walk to the northern cliffs adds two more hours to the bushwhack.

Valleys in the Harrisburg Quadrangle

THERE IS ONE more characteristic that distinguishes the Wilcox Lake Wild Forest Area from other parts of the Adirondacks: the relatively small number of lakes and ponds. The ponds are distinctively shallow, filling only fractions of the long valleys. Their outlets are often slow-moving streams. They are the remnants of glacial and post-glacial lakes that occupied all of the valleys. As the ice melted, the receding waters left the sand and gravel soil that fill the valleys and the eskers and drummonds that make ridges and small hills. The ponds, entrapments of melted water, continue to shrink in size, as does any natural body of water over the years.

This description is best exemplified by the valleys of Madison, Stewart, and East Stony creeks. Long, level sand barrens scarcely support more than scrubby cover. The sandy subsoil provides such good drainage that the ponds are shallow and and the soil is dry. The marshes are fields of reeds and rushes. These give way to dry fields that are only a few feet higher in elevation than the marshes. This is where the blueberries thrive.

Balsam pioneer these fields and then give way to a climax forest of spruce and pine. Because there is little calcium in the soil, the soil is naturally acid. Pines prefer this acid soil, and their needles further contribute to the soil's acidity. This restricts the undergrowth to acid-loving ferns and blueberries, with huge clumps of twinflower crowning mossy hillocks.

Slow-moving streams in such long valleys suggest great still-water canoeing. However, summer waters are often so low that they are canoeable only where beaver have dammed them to raise water levels. Some of the best potential streams require difficult carries.

The shallow ponds and beaver dams have one unpleasant drawback: they are filled with leeches, and so there are few good places to swim.

55 The Hub at Baldwin Springs
Camping, canoeing, picknicking, berrying

West Stony Creek Road reaches a T, 7.6 miles from Harrisburg Road. A right fork takes you to a ford over the East Stony Creek and to a loop into a pine grove. A fireplace and picnic tables make a perfect place to camp or plan a day's exploration of the pine barrens and the many trails, or to rest while picking the enormous quantities of blueberries that thrive nearby. If beaver have not flooded the ford, you will find an iron beam serves as a bridge across the creek. If it is flooded, use the bridge 0.3 mile south to cross the creek to the hub of trails.

You can reach six trails from the hub, which is officially called Baldwin Springs after the spring 0.2 mile north of the ford. It is in the midst of an open sand barrens covered with a sedge meadow. Long ago, someone surrounded the spring with a huge hollow log. Beaver dammed the outlet of the spring and created a pool, which is now a small grassy vly.

56 Indian Pond Loop
Marked snowmobile trail, hiking, skiing
5 miles circular, 3 hours, 80-foot vertical rise

Part of this trail is a great short walk, barely 1 mile each way to Stone Dam on Madison Creek and back from the trailhead 0.2 mile west of the Barber place. It becomes truly spectacular as a part of a 5-mile circuit from that trailhead or from the Hub at Baldwin Springs with the addition of a 1.7-mile walk along the West Stony Creek Road.

The stone dam that created Indian Pond is breached; the pond is no more. There is only a gentle, narrow flow through a huge grassy vly. The pond is all that remains of a glacial lake that stretched almost to Garnet Lake. Now, that two-and-a-half-mile-long valley is filled with marshes and the meandering stream. The valley is so level that the dam, never more than two feet high, created a 1-mile-long pond.

The walk to the dam is a joy in itself, for the route has several sections rich with balsam and delightfully scented. Most of the trail is in a pine barrens, with pines so tall that even a slight wind turns their whispering

Indian Pond on Madison Creek Flow

into the din of a superhighway. The route is marked with red disks. Two hundred yards from the start, it intersects an old road that leads back to the Barber place. Your way left is obvious and you will reach the dam after a twenty-five minute walk.

As seen from the dam, Mt. Blue looms over the meadows. A short walk along the western edge of the vly brings views to the northeast toward Crane Mountain, 7 miles away. Crane hangs majestically over the sea of waving grasses and rushes

From the western end of the dam, the red-marked trail heads south along the creek for 100 feet, then angles uphill through a draw filled with noble pine. As you approach the height-of-land, watch for the stump of a giant of that species, twice the diameter of those that grow here now. In fifteen minutes you cross the ridge and begin a fairly steep descent down the western slope. You will be impressed by the size of a clump of birch to the south of the trail. Twenty minutes from the dam you descend to the marshy valley that surrounds one of the outlets of Lixard Creek. A well-placed beaver dam makes crossing the creek possible. You climb an esker on the west side and revel in the balsam and tamarack with blueberries and crunchy lichens underfoot.

You reach the Lixard Pond Trail at 1.8 miles, though the sign says 1.6. It points north to that pond, section 57, and south to Baldwin Springs your route. Beyond a glacial erratic, you cross a small stream, the outlet of marshes to the northwest. The clearings grow larger, as do the tamarack that dot them. A ten-minute walk takes you 0.7 mile to another intersection, this one with the Fish Ponds Trail of section 58. Just beyond, you cross another tributary of Madison Creek and at 0.8 mile you intersect the Oregon Trail. The ford is straight ahead, the snowmobile bridge 0.3 mile to the south along the East Stony Creek.

From the bridge walk back north 0.3 mile, then west 1.7 miles along the road to the trailhead.

In spite of the fact you cannot drive to the trailhead in winter, you can enjoy Madison Creek Flow and a part of this trail, although it is a difficult ski trek.

Beaver have kept at the dam-building business, and a dam they constructed several years ago to the north, at a place natives call the real "Injun Pond," flooded the trail from Garnet Lake to Stone Dam. Now a summer walk this way is no longer possible; the trail is almost grown in or filled with deadfalls, and a bushwhack involves crossing alder meadows, flooded meadows, and spruce-covered eskers.

SKI LOOP THROUGH MADISON CREEK FLOW

A winter ski loop from Garnet Lake through Madison Creek Flow is a 9-mile run that will challenge any wilderness skier. It crosses the lake to its southern tip and bushwhacks to the valley by following the valley of the inlet stream. (An alternate using the abandoned snowmobile trail, section 49, is not recommended because of the number of blowdowns.)

A route southwest through the valley winds over eskers that separate patches of frozen marsh. In the north the marshes are often filled with alders. Conifers fill some swamps and densely cover the eskers. Only the last mile to the Stone Dam is a run through open snow fields beside the creek's meanders. To complete the loop, you would use the western part of this trail and return to Garnet Lake by way of Lixard Pond (see next section).

The trailless portion from Garnet Lake south to the meadows along the creek is arduous. This is a trek for strong skiers only.

Beaver meadow on Indian Pond Trail loop

57 Baldwin Springs to Lixard Pond and Garnet Lake

Marked snowmobile trail, skiing, hiking
4.3 miles one way, 2½ hours, minimal vertical rise

Add 0.6 mile to distances given for this walk if you are starting from the east side of the East Stony Creek. That accounts for the detour to cross the creek on the bridge rather than at the ford.

This trail makes exceptionally good summer walking as well as fine cross-country skiing. If you add this to any of the other spokes that meet at the Hub at Baldwin Springs, you have a fairly long walk. The walking is good, partly because it follows an old road, but mostly because of the handsome woods that border the trail.

From the west side of the East Stony Creek, walk north for 0.1 mile to the guideboards, which indicate the way east is the Oregon Trail and the way north is the route to Fish Ponds. Take the north route for another 0.1 mile to a fork and continue right, northeast. Here a sign indicates the distance, 4.1 miles, to Garnet Lake, and 0.7 mile to Indian Pond Junction.

Walking along these flats you enjoy views of Mt. Blue and its open rock summit. Even at 3.5 miles distant, the mountain dominates the sand barrens. Old logging roads and new jeep trails score the fields, which are edged with stands of lacy tamarack and blue-white balsam. The balsam are full and beautifully shaped as if designed for Christmas trees. There really is something special about the balsam. When that species grows under ideal conditions of soil and light, as it does here, the rows of needles are not thin and flat, but grow all around the end branches. Natives call these "double balsam," but they are just unusually beautiful specimens of the familiar species.

It is a ten-minute walk to the junction, where you take the left fork, continuing beneath a cover of enormous pines. The trail draws close 0.3 mile farther, at 1.2 miles, to one of the headwater streams of the East Stony Creek. The trail will follow this stream to Lixard Pond. Gradually the forest changes from pine to mixed spruce and hemlock. The stream cuts through a small valley shaded with hemlock and maple and birch. The trail continues on the west side of the valley for 1.4 miles, then crosses the small freshet that drains the tiny pond high on the shoulder of Mt. Blue.

The trail crosses a wet area from which the stream flows. In high-water times, the stream is really an outlet of Lixard Pond. You reach the pond at 2.9 miles and walk along it before descending to Garnet Lake at 4.3 miles.

58 Baldwin Springs to Fish Ponds to Bartman Trailhead

Marked snowmobile trail, skiing, hiking
6.6 miles one way, 3 to 3½ hours, 550-foot vertical rise

A direct trail to Fish Ponds from Baldwin Springs is one of the six routes that intersect at the springs, and it can be combined with one of the others for a long summer hike, or better, a winter ski trek.

In the field adjacent to the west side of the ford across the East Stony Creek, there are two guideboards, one pointing to the Oregon Trail and the other indicating the trail north to Fish Ponds, 3.7 miles away. Take the north route and continue on it where the Garnet Lake Trail forks to the northeast.

The roadway is broad and open, showing more signs that vehicles have used it than that anyone has walked it. The trail has been cleared better than when this guide was first written, but it is still not a very exciting walk. A very gentle uphill takes you to a draw, a short ascent, and at 1.9 miles a height-of-land. The trail continues its northern course, descending less than 200 feet in 0.8 mile to intersect the trail from Bartman Road to North Bend, section 37. You may not spot the intersection and will only be aware you have passed it as the trail direction changes to east of north. At 3.7 miles the trail approaches the southern end of Fish Ponds.

59 Stewart Creek Flow

Canoeing or skiing

Sportsmen have made use of those times when it is possible to drive from Baldwin Springs to North Bend and have carried row boats or canoes to the creek. It is often possible to find a boat secreted near North Bend. Without this access, you must be prepared to carry a canoe either from Bartman Trailead, 1.6 miles downhill; the Oregon Trail, 1 mile; or Baldwin Springs, 1.8 miles uphill.

If you are up to these carries, then you may be up to the one good, long canoe route in this region. The trip is susceptible to water variations and beaver constructions. The mileages are estimates of the stream's meanders. You can canoe 1.5 miles from the northern of the Fish Ponds to the intersection of its outlet with the southern one. Together they wind and twist southwest for 3 direct miles to North Bend, but the actual canoeable route is nearly twice that long. The water between the marshy shores is just open enough to float a canoe and two paddlers. The creek drops only six feet in the entire distance between Fish Ponds and the snowmobile bridge at North Bend. Within sight of the bridge, and upstream, there is a shallow stretch, 100 feet long, with no more than an inch or two of water in dry times.

Around North Bend, in a 1.5-mile loop through an oxbow meadow, the stream is so open that it is navigable by rowboat. Downstream, there is 0.25 mile of rapids that must be portaged, but at both ends there is fairly easy access to the Oregon Trail. Below the rapids, there is another 1.5 miles through flowed lands and alder swamps where the creek drops scarcely at all. At the snowmobile bridge, the gentle, floating trip is over and there is another 1-mile carry to NY 8.

Skiing the flows along Stewart Creek can be as much fun as exploring Madison Creek Flow, as long as you are cautious. The wet marshes beside the creek freeze solid and support a good snow cover. Where the creek is sluggish, it, too, often freezes solid. However, there is no need to risk finding spots of open water, with the miles of safe, frozen marsh. If in doubt, stay close to the clumps of alders and other shrubs pushing through the snow. Also, if you run into bad conditions, the snowmobile trail follows the flow on safe ground for the entire length.

Harrisburg and the East Stony Creek Valley

ONE OF THE most inviting roads in the area, one that should lead to all kinds of adventures, turns out to have mixed attributes. On the one hand, it is a beautiful drive through the valley to Harrisburg on a road that becomes impassable to ordinary vehicles after a dozen miles. The valley is broad and deep, sheltered with mountain ranges on either side and filled with many small farms. Baldhead Mountain, with its bare, rocky summit, dominates the skyline when you make the return drive northeast from Harrisburg.

The USGS map suggests several old roads and trails for hiking, all originating in the valley, however both sides of the road are private and almost all of the land is posted so there is limited access. The exception is a small sliver of state land touching the road at a state parking area, 3.1 miles west of Wolf Pond Road. There is no trail to state lands south of the parking area, but one does go north. It leads 0.5 mile uphill to state land— a great access for hunters—but it ends at state land. Nevertheless, it crosses a lovely stream and marsh and has become popular with fishermen and birders. Note that because of intervening private land it can not be used to reach Little Pond as advertised in some local brochures.

Two trails lead from the section of road beyond Harrisburg Lake. The Lodge at Harrisburg Lake is an attractive place to stay. In recent years, skiers have made special arrangements to stay there midway through a long ski trip from the Hope Valley, section 15, to NY 8 at Oregon. Winter may be the best time to find recreation opportunities here.

While hikers should avoid the valley in hunting season, enjoyment of it at other times will be limited by the extensive use of motorized vehicles on trails, even where it is prohibited. The fact that people drive the Harrisburg Road as far as Wilcox Lake ford, and beyond to the lake when the ford is not flooded, detracts from this approach to the lake. The ruts

will remind you of Barney Fowler's humorous story in his *Adirondack Album*. He recounted the adventures of a three-and-a-half-ton trailer rig that "strayed" down the road, past dead end signs, in snow and darkness, looking for a shortcut west. You will marvel that the rig did not jackknife before it did, almost at the Wilcox Lake ford, and you will be appalled to see that trucks still drive this route all the way to the ford.

60 Harrisburg Lake to Bakertown to Wilcox Lake

Marked snowmobile trail
4.9 miles one way, 2½ hours, 200-foot vertical rise

You probably will not want to walk this way to Wilcox Lake unless you are interested in the shortest and easiest route and have no care for scenery on the way. A winter trek might be more enticing. In summer, the distance can be shortened by driving west of Harrisburg Lake. Ordinary vehicles can drive for 1.5 miles or so, but it is not recommended. As noted, four-wheel-drive vehicles go much farther.

A sign at the causeway at Harrisburg Lake says "500 lb limit." Everyone seems to ignore this. You will see people camping on the shore west of the causeway, though this is private land. The road heads generally west, passing the old trailhead for Baldwin Springs at 0.8 mile. You reach state land at 1.25 miles. There is a place to camp in a clearing 250 yards farther west. The road deterioriates significantly beyond this point. A sharp downhill brings you at 1.9 miles to the trailhead to Baldwin Springs.

At 2.6 miles, you reach a snowmobile bridge over the outlet of Harrisburg Lake. A cement ford beside the bridge allows vehicles to continue. The road swings southwest and reaches the area known as Bakertown, an abandoned logging settlement. At 2.9 miles you cross to private land of the Moosewood Club, a group hunting camp. Their large private inholding explains the use of vehicles this far. The road traverses the private land for 0.7 mile.

There is no indication that you return to state land, but 0.3 mile farther, at 3.9 miles, you pass the pine-covered knoll that marks the ford. Crossing here is a question of how much of the East Stony Creek is flooded by beaver activity. You continue south for 0.3 mile to the snowmobile bridge

Bridge over Stony Creek

and a safe crossing. From here it is 0.7 mile to Wilcox Lake.

The entire route is through forests that have been disturbed by logging in the not-too-distant past. Signs of abandoned settlements are everywhere, even in the stretch between the ford and the bridge where the trail crosses open fields.

61 The Arrow Trail from Baldwin Springs to Harrisburg Lake

Marked snowmobile trail, cross-country skiing
7.5 miles one way, 3 hours, minimal vertical rise

The Arrow Trail follows the East Stony Creek Valley from Baldwin Springs to the extension of the Harrisburg Road. The only time you can drive to the trailheads is in summer, at a time when the route is not very exciting for hikers. Even then, most people could not drive right to the southern trailhead, so the distance given is short by 0.5 mile or more.

In winter, this is a great ski route, but you would have to make a very long ski trek to reach Baldwin Springs and add at least 1.9 miles to the distance to reach the end of the plowed road at Harrisburg Lake. Other ski trips that take advantage of this long, level route are so long that you would need either to camp along the way, or to make arrangements to break the trip by staying at Harrisburg Lodge.

From Baldwin Springs, head south on the road, passing the snowmobile bridge over the East Stony Creek at 0.3 mile and reaching private land around the Dog and Pup Club at Fullers at 0.7 mile. Continue on the roadway through the property. The trail crosses the Madison Creek at 1.3 miles—no bridge and a possible messy crossing. A snowmobile by-pass to the left has been abandoned since the right-of-way across the private land has been established. You will probably not even notice it now. You continue straight ahead at the Forest Preserve sign.

The road, which has so far been in very good condition, shows little evidence of use, except for the treads of three-wheel ATVs. You are never far from the meadows which surround the creek, but never close enough to see them well. Balsam, spruce, and pine give way to an open forest of hardwoods as the trail rounds Wolf Point Mountain.

Wilcox Lake

There are several ranges of cliffs on Wolf Point Mountain and the unnamed mountain to its south. The latter is visible from the causeway at the outlet of Harrisburg Lake. You would use this trail to begin a bushwhack to either of them, so the distances involved are great.

You reach a snowmobile bridge over Hill Creek at 4.1 miles, and the walking is so easy it will take as little as an hour and a quarter to cover that distance. The trail climbs about 100 feet above the valley and continues south, following the old road for another 2 miles, a forty-minute walk. The road continues straight ahead at the junction at 6.1 miles and quickly reaches private land denoted by yellow blazes. Snowmobiles continue to use this shorter route, apparently with the permission of the landowner, but because the state has no legal access, no trail is marked along the roadway. The roadway reaches Harrisburg Road in 0.7 mile at an unmarked intersection that is 0.8 mile west of the causeway over Harrisburg Lake.

The right fork to the west, is rougher, narrower, rocky, and slower walking. The trail is the left fork, marked by an arrow. It descends the north shoulder of another knob and reaches another intersection in 0.8 mile. The trail, again, is a left fork, marked by an arrow, following an old roadway. You climb slightly, then descend reaching Harrisburg Road 1.9 miles west of the causeway, completing the circuitous 1.4 miles and forty-minute detour around private land.

In addition to skiing the trail, you can ski the frozen marshes along the East Stony Creek. Then you will see not only broad views of the valley, but the splendid stands of balsam, spruce, and tamarack that are filling it.

62 Canoeing the Upper East Stony Creek

In early spring, considerably more of this route is canoeable than in low summer waters. There is less than a 100-foot drop in the East Stony Creek between the end of the West Stony Creek Road and Bakertown. In high water, the entire 7-mile stretch can be canoed by whitewater enthusiasts. Even in low water, those who prefer flat water can find several long, placid stretches.

There is a small rapids south of Fullers, which you can avoid by putting your canoe in below the confluence of Madison Creek. To do this, you have to carry south from Fullers. There is only one more portage, which separates a beaver flow from the 2.5 miles of gently flowing stream on the south. Depending on the water level, you can either walk through the rapids, floating your canoe beside you, or carry on the high ground of the trail.

Southwest of Stony Creek, the Lens Lake Valley

BECAUSE OF ITS proximity to the Hudson River and the railroad, Stony Creek grew throughout the latter part of the nineteenth century to become a vital center for logging and tanning. Today, you will find many tourist accommodations, especially ranches for horseback riding. Almost all of the roadsides south and west of Stony Creek are privately owned. The road past Lens Lake continues on to extensive private paper company holdings. There are only small sections along the road that are state land, but these offer two very easy nature adventures that you won't want to miss.

63 Lens Lake

Canoeing, picnicking

A quaking bog is one of nature's most fascinating places, and Lens Lake is one of the Adirondacks' most accessible bogs. It is easy to explore the lake and its bogs with a canoe, and you can spend a day paddling, photographing, and simply observing.

The Lens Lake/Roaring Brook Road is the western road at the four corners in Stony Creek. Turn left on Lens Lake Road at 3.3 miles. The right turn to Lens Lake is just over 2 miles farther. You can park near the lake and easily launch a canoe.

A mat of sphagnum, the mark of a quaking bog, covers more than half of the surface of the lake. The bog surrounds all of the shores and covers so much of the north end of the lake that only a few small channels there are navigable by canoe.

The lake is an superb wildlife and nature sanctuary. In summer you should see many ducks in the concealed bays in the north. Great blue heron have

roosted there. Water lilies cover most of the open water, and their August bloom turns the surface snowy white.

The sphagnum bog is home to sundew and pitcher plants, cranberries and sweet gale, bladderworts and pipeworts—all the strange plants that survive only in a bog. In the spring there are wild calla, cotton grass, bog rosemary, Labrador tea, and swamp laurel. The sphagnum mat, with its growing surface on top of the floating mass of dead plants, is two to seven feet thick and is gradually filling in the lake.

It takes nearly three hours to paddle all around the edges of the bog and through the channels. You can spend most of a day photographing stumps, plants, and bugs. For years I tried to capture an insect in the clutches of the dewy hairs that surround sundew leaves. However, the leaves are small and the bugs proportionately smaller, so that even my best efforts with a close-up lens were a disappointment until one day at Lens Lake I found a small, silvery blue damsel fly, still alive, but ensnared by a sundew leaf holding and digesting each of the insect's wings, with a third leaf grasping its long tail.

64 Middle Flow
Canoeing, camping

If you continue down the road past Lens Lake, the road passes for a time through Forest Preserve land, then private lands begin again on the south. You cross the outlet of Middle Flow, 1.4 miles from the Lens Lake access. You can launch a canoe from the causeway and explore this 0.75-mile-long pond. It is very shallow and fills its current length only because the outlet dam has been repaired, by both man and beaver. South of the dam there is a site used by campers; just beyond, the road enters private and posted property.

Middle Flow is peppered with stumps and boulders, but some of the accessible shoreline is covered with spruce and hemlock. The northwest shore and all of Wheeler Mountain beyond are Forest Preserve lands.

South of Stony Creek, More Open Peaks

SARATOGA COUNTY'S TOWN of Hadley lies south of Stony Creek. A marvelous range of mountains known by the ancient Indian name, Kayaderossera, crosses the township and dips down to the Sacandaga valley. These mountains are the southern foothills of the Adirondacks.

The lowlands of the township were settled before the revolution and the slopes have been repeatedly logged. In the nineteenth century, the forests supplied many sawmills throughout the town and very large tanneries at Conklingville and Luzerne. Most of the township is still made up of large timber tracts. Almost all of its land is privately owned. The town has only small parcels of public land in the north, near the border with Stony Creek, but they are enough to offer three good adventures. Its principal mountain, Hadley, is one of the highlights of this guide.

65 Wolf Creek Road
Walking, skiing

A small, shallow, man-made pond is formed by a dam on Wolf Creek near the intersection of the creek and Hadley Tower Road. To find the place, head south of Stony Creek on Hadley Road, turn west on Riley Hill Road, and in 2.5 miles turn right to Hadley Tower Road. Turn right again in 0.6 mile at an unmarked intersection. There is a dirt road on the southeast of the pond leading toward the dam and a charming picnic site, from which the views of Roundtop and Hadley are impressive.

On the west of the pond, another old road heads north along Wolf Creek through private but unposted lands to state land. This route was marked as a snowmobile trail through to Waite Road, which is just south of Stony Creek, but it is no longer so marked. In fact the beginning of the route is obliterated and so is one of the handsomest and most accessible stands of hemlock in the Adirondacks. Many enjoyed the old road as a short nature walk, and recommended that the state acquire the area. This was not done, and shortly after this guide was last revised, the stand was logged. You can still walk north along the old road, though there are confusing side logging roads branching from it and the road has none of the wonderful charm of the past.

If you can follow the roadway north to state land, you can still enjoy a short nature walk, however, for the borders of the creek are home to many wildflowers and ferns. The roadway crosses the creek to state land at 0.6 mile and recrosses it to private land at 1.8 miles. The middle stretch remains a special place, even if the southern end is so disturbed.

66 Hadley Mountain

Marked trail
4 miles round trip, 3 hours, 1550-foot vertical rise

A marker at the foot of Hadley Mountain gives grim reminder of the reasons for the tower on its summit. The state marker at the trailhead says, "Successive fires in 1903, 1908, 1911, and 1915 severely burned 12,000 acres of the surrounding forest land." The nearly bare summit of the whole West Mountain ridge, of which Hadley, at just under 2700 feet elevation, is the southern peak, gives testimony to the damages to forest and soil. There is no better view in the southern Adirondacks. The open peak permits the enjoyment of the spectacular panorama without even a climb to the tower, which is still manned.

The trailhead is 1.5 miles south on Hadley Tower Road, section 65. From the south, Hadley Tower Road is a left turn north from Hadley Hill Road, which connects Day Center on the Great Sacandaga Lake with the Hadley/Stony Creek Road.

The trail starts with a continuous climb southwest to the ridge line. The fires that burned the hillside also consumed the topsoil, so only a thin cover has accumulated on the smooth gneiss base. As a result, the steepest, most worn part of the trail is over a "sidewalk" of smooth rock. The forest cover contains pioneering species of birch and popple, viburnum and striped

View from Hadley Mountain

maple, and mountain ash. At 1.2 miles the trail levels out briefly, turning north of west to follow the ridge. Near the summit, the trail heads west to approach from the south.

Only the view to the west past Spruce Mountain is at all restricted, for Hadley seems to stand alone. The view south is across the Great Sacandaga Lake, past the Mohawk Valley and the Helderbergs, to some of the Catskill's higher peaks. To the northwest, lie Bearpen and Mt. Blue. To the north, beyond Roundtop, many of the High Peaks are visible between Crane, Baldhead, and Moose. Nippletop and Dix are easily identified. To the east, Three Sisters, Moon, and other hills by the Hudson lie in front of the Willsboro Range, which edges Lake Champlain. Beyond Pharaoh Mountain are the Green Mountains stretching north to south as far as the eye can see. On a clear day, Hadley's horizons seem boundless.

67 Roundtop

Bushwhack to an open peak

A really full day of walking results from adding a bushwhack to Roundtop to the climb to Hadley. The bushwhack can be a round-trip loop from the summit of Hadley or it can add a descent of the east face of Roundtop to the old road on the west side of Wolf Creek, section 65.

On the bushwhack over to Roundtop, it is easier to walk to the west of and below the ridge connecting it to Hadley, taking a course a little

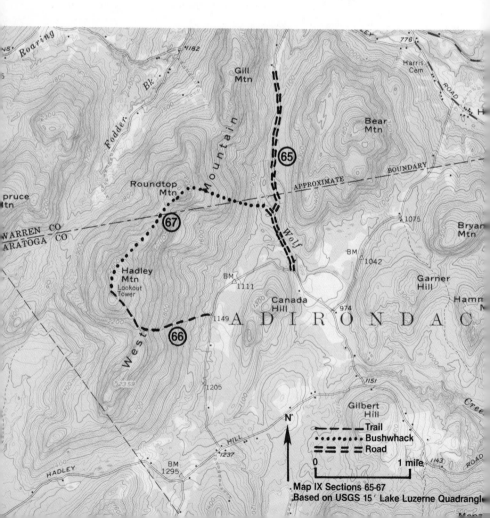

Map IX Sections 65-67
Based on USGS 15' Lake Luzerne Quadrangle

east of northeast and picking out open and bare rock areas along the way. The walking is occasionally brushy, but there are quite a few open patches where only lichens grow, crunching underfoot like popcorn. Several places offer views along the long, gentle slope down to the saddle between the peaks. Be careful to stay near the top of the ridge and use glimpses of Roundtop's summit to guide when possible. The col at 2200 feet ends the descent of 450 feet in 1 mile and can be reached from Hadley in under an hour's walk.

The approach to Roundtop from the saddle is blocked with several series of low cliffs ranging up the 200-foot climb to the summit from the col. However, it is easy to find a way around the ends of the cliffs. The open summit sweeps down to the northeast with views nearly as fine as those from Hadley, but infinitely more private. To the west, there is a precipitous drop seemingly straight down to Wolf Creek Pond, with a view farther east to the Hudson.

If you choose the round-trip walk back to Hadley, allow at least three hours for the loop from Hadley's summit.

If a more adventurous route is desired, the bushwhack down to the road along Wolf Creek takes less than an hour and a half from Roundtop, but it does require some experience. Descend to the north of the series of steep cliffs on Roundtop's eastern face, picking up the top of the obvious ridge and setting a course of barely south of east. This way, the steepest cliffs will be to the right, or south, during the descent. However, there are still half a dozen ledges that require careful climbing over the talus and huge fallen boulders. This is a wild and dramatic series of ledges, the most unusual of which is a 400-foot-long wall of rock, several feet thick and separated from the mountainside proper by a ravine a foot and a half wide that varies up to fifteen feet in depth.

With luck, it is possible to pick up the brushy ends of one of the skid roads and use it as it is funneled toward the main logging road, which leads to the Wolf Creek Road. In any event, the stream, the road, and the valley are guide enough to assure an easy outlet to Hadley Tower Road.

References and Other Resources

References

Aber, Ted. *Adirondack Folks.* Prospect, NY: Prospect Books, 1980.

Aber, Ted, and Stella King. *The History of Hamilton County.* Lake Pleasant, NY: Great Wilderness Books, 1965.

Girard, Ouida. *Ghost Town in the Adirondacks and Other Tales.* Privately printed, 1980.

Simms, Jeptha R. *Trappers of New York.* Albany, NY: J. Munsell, 1857. Reprint. Harrison, NY: Harbor Hill Books, 1984.

Whipple, Janice, M. *Stony Creek Then & Now.* Stony Creek, NY: Stony Creek Historical Association, 1980.

Other Resources

New York State Department of Environmental Conservation (DEC) 50 Wolf Road, Albany, New York 12233

For plants:
DEC List of Rare and Endangered Plants

For trails:
DEC Brochure, *Nordic Skiing and Snowshoeing Trails*
DEC Regional Office, Warrensburg, New York 12885
DEC Regional Office, Northville, New York 12134
Adirondack Mountain Club, 172 Ridge Street, Glens Falls, New York 12801

For other things to do in the Adirondacks:
New York State Department of Commerce, Albany, New York 12245, "I Love New York" series: *Camping, Tourism Map, State Travel Guide.*

Index

Guidebooks from The Countryman Press and Backcountry Publications

Written for people of all ages and experience, these popular and carefully prepared books feature detailed trail and tour directions, notes on points of interest and natural phenomena, maps and photographs.

Walks and Rambles Series
Walks and Rambles on the Delmarva
   Peninsula, $9.95
Walks and Rambles in Dutchess and Putnam
   Counties (NY), $9.95
Walks and Rambles in Rhode Island, $9.95
Walks and Rambles in the Upper Connecticut
   River Valley, $9.95
Walks and Rambles in Westchester (NY) and
   Fairfield (CT) Counties, $8.95

Biking Series
25 Mountain Bike Tours in Vermont, $9.95
25 Bicycle Tours on Delmarva, $8.95
25 Bicycle Tours in Eastern Pennsylvania,
   $8.95
20 Bicycle Tours in the Finger Lakes, $8.95
20 Bicycle Tours in the 5 Boroughs (NYC),
   $8.95
25 Bicycle Tours in the Hudson Valley, $9.95
25 Bicycle Tours in Maine, $9.95
25 Bicycle Tours in New Hampshire, $7.95
25 Bicycle Tours in New Jersey, $8.95
20 Bicycle Tours in and around New York City,
   $7.95
25 Bicycle Tours in Vermont, $8.95

Canoeing Series
Canoe Camping Vermont and New Hampshire
   Rivers, $7.95
Canoeing Central New York, $10.95
Canoeing Massachusetts, Rhode Island and
   Connecticut, $7.95

Hiking Series
50 Hikes in the Adirondacks, $11.95
50 Hikes in Central New York, $9.95
50 Hikes in Central Pennsylvania, $9.95
50 Hikes in Eastern Pennsylvania, $10.95

50 Hikes in the Hudson Valley, $10.95
50 Hikes in Massachusetts, $11.95
50 More Hikes in New Hampshire, $9.95
50 Hikes in New Jersey, $10.95
50 Hikes in Northern Maine, $10.95
50 Hikes in Ohio, $12.95
50 Hikes in Southern Maine, $10.95
50 Hikes in Vermont, $11.95
50 Hikes in West Virginia, $9.95
50 Hikes in Western New York, $12.95
50 Hikes in Western Pennsylvania, $11.95
50 Hikes in the White Mountains, $12.95

Adirondack Series
Discover the Adirondack High Peaks, $14.95
Discover the Central Adirondacks, $8.95
Discover the Eastern Adirondacks, $9.95
Discover the Northeastern Adirondacks, $9.95
Discover the Northern Adirondacks, $10.95
Discover the Northwestern Adirondacks, $12.95
Discover the South Central Adirondacks, $10.95
Discover the Southeastern Adirondacks, $9.95
Discover the Southern Adirondacks, $10.95
Discover the Southwestern Adirondacks, $9.95
Discover the West Central Adirondacks, $13.95

Ski-Touring Series
25 Ski Tours in Central New York, $8.95
25 Ski Tours in New Hampshire, $8.95
25 Ski Tours in Vermont, $8.95

Other Guides
Maine: An Explorer's Guide, $14.95
New England's Special Places, $12.95
New Jersey's Special Places, $12.95
New York State's Special Places, $12.95
Pennsylvania Trout Streams and their Hatches,
   $14.95
Vermont: An Explorer's Guide, $16.95
Waterfalls of the White Mountains, $14.95

The above titles are available at bookstores and at certain sporting goods stores or may be ordered directly from the publisher. For complete descriptions of these and other guides, write: The Countryman Press, P.O. Box 175, Woodstock, VT 05091.